INTERNATIONAL EDITION

LIBRARYSPEAK

a glossary of terms in librarianship
and information management

Compiled by
Lynn Farkas

TotalRecall Publications, Inc..
1103 Middlecreek
Friendswood, Texas 77546
281-992-3131   281-482-5390 Fax
www.totalrecallpress.com

All rights reserved. Except as permitted under the United States Copyright Act of 1976, No part of this publication may be reproduced, stored in a retrieval system, or transmitted in any form or by any means electronic or mechanical or by photocopying, recording, or otherwise without prior permission of the publisher. Exclusive worldwide content publication / distribution by TotalRecall Publications, Inc.

Copyright © 2015 by Lynn Farkas
Based on the original works by Mary Mortimer

ISBN: 978-1-59095-442-3
UPC: 6-43977-44424-0

Printed in the United States of America with simultaneous printings in Australia, Canada, and United Kingdom.

FIRST EDITION
1 2 3 4 5 6 7 8 9 10

Library of Congress Control Number: 2014955312

Judgments as to the suitability of the information herein is the purchaser's responsibility. TotalRecall Publications, Inc. extends no warranties, makes no representations, and assumes no responsibility as to the accuracy or suitability of such information for application to the purchaser's intended purposes or for consequences of its use except as described herein.

The scanning, uploading and distribution of this book via the Internet or via any other means without the permission of the publisher is illegal and punishable by law. Please purchase only authorized electronic editions and do not participate in or encourage electronic piracy of copyrighted materials. Your support of the author's rights is appreciated.

LibrarySpeak is dedicated to every librarian and every library studies student who struggles with the traditional language of librarianship.

About the Author

Author **Lynn Farkas** is a librarian, library trainer and director of an information services consulting company. Her expertise includes subject analysis, thesaurus development, knowledge management applications, metadata and database indexing. She has studied and worked in libraries in America and Australia, and taught in Australia, Asia and the Pacific. She knows the terminology and organizations of these areas and brings that experience to the compilation of this glossary.

About the Book

LibrarySpeak provides simple definitions for all the terms required by professional and paraprofessional library workers. Comprehensive definitions can be found in other sources, but *LibrarySpeak* provides an accessible and convenient quick reference.

This first international edition consolidates earlier North American and Australasian editions of *LibrarySpeak* into one volume. It contains over 2000 words, phrases, acronyms, and national and international organizations and programs which everyone in the library world needs to know.

This is a reference book which should be in the hands of every library student, and every library and library classroom should have at least one copy.

About the Learn Library Skills Series

Other essential library texts from TotalRecall include workbooks in *the Learn Library Skills* Series: Learn About Information, Learn Basic Library Skills, Learn Cataloguing the RDA Way, Learn DDC 23rd edition, Learn Library Management, Learn Library of Congress Classification, Learn Library of Congress Subject Access, and Learn Reference Work.

Introduction

Librarianship is one of many areas of work in which everyday exchanges include technical language, acronyms and abbreviations. Students in library courses and new library staff daily encounter terms, references and acronyms that they need to understand. As the scope of librarianship expands, even 'old hands' frequently encounter new terminology.

LibrarySpeak defines key terms and describes major organizations involved with librarianship. New formats of material—e.g., graphic novels, manga—and new library initiatives—e.g., Trove, Bibframe—are defined and explained. New technical language appears every day, particularly in computer-based industries, and key terms that are important for library operations are noted.

This edition also includes comprehensive terminology for the new **Resource Description and Access** (RDA) cataloging standard, and identifies new terms and concepts—e.g., institutional repositories and discovery layer software—that apply to electronic resources.

There have been many changes to the library scene since the last edition of *LibrarySpeak*. Organizations have changed name or ceased operation, and new ones have taken their place. Global cooperation among libraries has increased, and while this edition continues to highlight North American and Australasian institutions, it also includes major international organizations and initiatives of interest to library workers in all countries.

LibrarySpeak contains URLs for sites on the Internet. They all exist at the time of writing. As all Internet users know, there are few guarantees that any (except PURLs) will still be there tomorrow, and I accept no responsibility for them. I have found the Net the fastest and easiest way to update information, especially about organizations, and think that you may use it in the same way.

There have also been some personnel changes to *LibrarySpeak*. Mary Mortimer, compiler of all the earlier editions, has retired and passed the mantle of compiler to me. She kindly allowed me to use her earlier texts as the basis for this edition, and I am grateful for her encouragement and support.

I am eager to continue revising *LibrarySpeak* on a regular basis, and welcome suggestions from its users. Please alert me to new terms, acronyms, usage and omissions, as your feedback is the best goad for keeping this work up-to-date.

Lynn Farkas
September 2014

How to Use LibrarySpeak

The glossary is designed so that you only have to look in one place. There are full definitions for each entry, whether it is a full name or initials, for example:
> **BL** British Library. The national library of the United Kingdom

and
> **British Library** BL. The national library of the United Kingdom

are both included as full entries.

The exceptions are obsolete terms, and a *See* reference refers you to the current term, for example:
> **National Library of Canada** *See* Library and Archives Canada

Alternative terms are listed at the beginning of the definition, for example:
> **book jacket** Also dust cover, dust jacket, dust wrapper, jacket, wrapper. Paper cover for a hard-bound book

The same definition is given under each term.

Where it is helpful to know about a related term, you are referred to it by the abbreviation **Cf**, for example:
> **authorized access point** In RDA cataloging, the preferred title or name to be used as an access point in a descriptive cataloging record. Cf variant access point

The terms are arranged in letter-by-letter alphabetical order. Many terms can be spelled either as a whole word, a hyphenated word or two words. Letter-by-letter arrangement does not change the order of the terms, whichever form you are looking for. For example
> **end matter**
> **endnote**
> **end papers**

are in this order, whether the terms are one word or two.

All initials are written without spaces or periods. This is not the practice of all organizations, but there are variant spacings in many terms, so it seems practical to standardize on one format.

This edition is designed for use across countries that employ different spelling conventions for English words. For consistency, American spelling has been adopted for the text of the glossary entries. Both American and English spelling are given for glossary headings, for example:
> **artifact, artefact** An object made by a person

LibrarySpeak

AACR2, AACR2R *Anglo-American Cataloguing Rules* Second edition, Second edition 2002 revision. A set of rules for descriptive cataloging adopted by libraries in English-speaking countries. Replaced by RDA (*Resource Description and Access*) in 2010

AALL American Association of Law Libraries. Organization of law librarians and related professionals, founded to develop law libraries and librarianship http://www.aallnet.org/

AAQ Association des Archivistes du Québec. An association that promotes services and professional development in French to Quebec archivists http://www.archivistes.qc.ca/

AARNet Australia's Research and Education Network. An electronic network of regional networks providing access to the Internet and electronic sharing of information to Australian universities and research agencies http://www.aarnet.edu.au/

Aboriginal & Torres Strait Islander Library, Information and Resource Network Inc. ATSILIRN. Established in 1993 to support Australian Aboriginal and Torres Strait Islander library and information workers, and to improve the way information professionals perceive the information needs of Aboriginal and Torres Strait Islander peoples http://aiatsis.gov.au/atsilirn/index.php

aboutness A concept in subject analysis that refers to the degree to which a document is about a particular topic

abridged edition, abridgement, abridgment A condensed form of a work

abstract Also summary. A brief indication of the essential points of an article or literary work

abstracting service A bibliographic service that provides summaries of periodical articles, conference papers and chapters of edited books

ACA Association of Canadian Archivists. An association founded in 1975, devoted to professional and research activities of Canadian archivists http://archivists.ca/

ACACC/ACMLA Association des Cartothèques et Archives Cartographiques du Canada / Association of Canadian Map Libraries and Archives. The professional organization for Canadian map librarians, cartographic archivists, and geographic information specialists
http://www.acmla.org/

academic freedom The idea that academics may research, teach, and disseminate knowledge without fear of reprisal

academic library A library serving the information needs of the students and staff of a university or similar institution

academic-special library An academic library specialising in a limited subject area—e.g., the medical library of a university's medical faculty

ACARM Association of Commonwealth Archivists and Records Managers. An organization that promotes the development of professional archival and records management standards in the Commonwealth
http://www.acarm.org/

ACBD/CALL Association Canadienne des Bibliothèques de Droit / Canadian Association of Law Libraries. An association that promotes law libraries and professional development in law librarianship in Canada
http://www.callacbd.ca/

ACC Australian Copyright Council. An independent non-profit organization that aims to increase copyright awareness and influence changes to law and policy to benefit creators and copyright owners
http://www.copyright.org.au

acceptable use policy Guidelines to control how library computers may be used, especially to access the Internet—e.g., some libraries do not allow games to be played, or to send or receive email

access To obtain information from an information agency or database

access code Also authorization code. A username and/or password that is typed by a user to gain access to a computer system, network, or database (e.g., student access to a university computer network)

Access Copyright The Canadian copyright licensing agency, a consortium that issues licenses and develops policies for copyright-protected works
http://www.accesscopyright.ca/

accession To record the particulars of each item as it is received in a library

accession number The unique number given to an item to record its addition to the library

accession record A record with details of the ordering and receipt of an item in a library

accessions 1. Additions to the library stock. 2. The process of accessioning library materials

accessions list A list showing additions to a library's collection

accessions register A list of all the items added to a collection in the order in which they are added

access point Any part of a catalog or database record, or entry in a bibliography, that enables a user to find the resource

access point control In RDA, the control of access points by establishing and using consistent headings

access services The provision of access to a library's resources, including circulation, document delivery, security, reshelving, and stack maintenance

access time Also response time. The time an online system takes to respond to a user's command. Cf turnaround time

Access to Information Act (Canada) Legislation enacted in 1985, giving the public the right of access to the information of federal government institutions
http://laws-lois.justice.gc.ca/eng/acts/A-1/

accredited library school In the U.S. and Canada, a teaching institution whose library program has been accepted by the American Library Association

ACER Australian Council for Educational Research. Independent educational research organization. Produces *Australian Education Index*
http://www.acer.edu.au

acid free paper Also durable paper, permanent paper. Paper that is pH neutral, and will last longer than paper with acid content

acidity Presence of acid in library material or containers, which causes the material to become brittle and eventually disintegrate

acid migration Movement of acid from a container to the item itself

acid paper Paper with sufficient acid content to cause paper to yellow and become brittle over time

acknowledgments, acknowledgements That part of a book where the author recognizes the contributions others have made to the work

ACMLA/ACACC Association of Canadian Map Libraries and Archives / Association des Cartothèques et Archives Cartographiques du Canada. The professional organization for Canadian map librarians, cartographic archivists, and geographic information specialists
http://www.acmla.org/

ACOC Australian Committee on Cataloguing. A joint committee of ALIA and the National Library of Australia, charged with monitoring and influencing developments in national and international cataloging and classification
http://www.nla.gov.au/acoc/about-us

acquisition number A unique number identifying an item on a purchase order

acquisitions 1. The process of adding to a library's collection by purchase, gift or exchange. 2. The material so added

acquisition services The section and procedures of a library concerned with ordering and receiving material. Usually part of technical services

acronym A word formed from the initials of the name of an organization, system or service, pronounced as a word. Cf initialism

Action for Development through Libraries Programme ALP. An IFLA program to further the library profession, library institutions and library and information services in developing countries
http://www.ifla.org/VI/1/alp.htm

adaptation A modification of a work, to suit a different group of readers, or in a different literary form or medium

adapter A person who rewrites another person's work

added copy A copy added to a library's collection of an item it already owns

added edition An edition of an item added to a collection, which differs from editions of the same title already present in the collection

added entry In AACR2, any entry, other than the main entry and subject entries, that represents the resource in the catalog. Cf main entry

addendum (Plural addenda) Matter added to a book after the type has been set

adhesive binding Also perfect binding. Binding in which the back edge of a volume is trimmed, and adhesive is applied before the case is attached

adjacency operator Also proximity operator. A word or symbol that enables searching of terms close to each other in a title etc. — e.g., near, with

adjustable shelving A shelving system in which each shelf can be detached and moved up or down on the uprights to house materials of varying height

advance copy 1. A copy of a work sent to a reviewer, bookseller, etc. before the work is available to the public. 2. A copy of a work bound before other copies to enable the publisher to check that it is complete and correct

Affiliate Assembly A body of representatives and delegates of organizations affiliated with a division of the American Library Association

agent 1. A person who represents the interests of an author. 2. A person commissioned by a publisher or distributor to sell books to retail outlets or information agencies

aggregator A supplier of electronic journals and/or databases that enables the user to subscribe to a set of titles which are then accessed through the supplier's website

AGIFT Australian Governments' Interactive Functions Thesaurus. A thesaurus that describes the business functions carried out across Commonwealth, state and local governments in Australia
http://agift.naa.gov.au

AGLIN Australian Government Libraries Information Network. A network of librarians in Australian government libraries, who aim to represent the interests of member libraries and information services, and to develop and implement cooperative schemes and resources
http://www.aglin.org/

AGLS Australian Government Locator Service. A set of metadata elements based on the Dublin Core Element Set, with minor variations to suit Australian Government requirements, used to describe Internet resources
http://www.agls.gov.au/

AGRIS A database and network supported by the FAO, containing references on agricultural research and technology as well as links to related data sources on the World Wide Web
http://agris.fao.org/

AILA American Indian Library Association. A group founded to address the library-related needs of American Indians and Alaska Natives
http://ailanet.org/

ALA American Library Association. Professional library organization of the United States that aims to support and promote libraries and the library profession. See their website for divisions, publications, awards and prizes
http://www.ala.org

ALA Offices 1. Units within the American Library Association that address broad interests and issues of concern to the profession and the Association. 2. Headquarters of ALA in Chicago

ALCC Australian Libraries Copyright Committee. A policy body of major Australian libraries and organizations, for the discussion of copyright issues affecting the library, archive and information sectors. It advocates for copyright law reform on behalf of libraries and copyright users
http://libcopyright.org.au/

ALED Australian Libraries: The Essential Directory. National printed directory of Australian academic, public, joint use and special libraries, and other information relevant to the library and information industry—e.g., associations, library suppliers etc.

ALIA Australian Library and Information Association. The professional association of Australian librarians, library technicians and organizations, whose aim is to support and promote libraries in the community. See their website for their interest groups, publications, awards and prizes
http://www.alia.org.au

ALISE Association for Library and Information Science Education. A U.S. organization founded in 1915, that promotes excellence in research, teaching, and service for library and information science education
http://www.alise.org/

allonym The name of a real person assumed as a pen name by another writer. Cf pseudonym

almanac 1. An annual calendar with astronomical information and other data. 2. A miscellany of useful facts and statistical information

ALMS Automated library management system. Also ILS, ILMS. An automated package of library services that contains several functions such as circulation, cataloging etc.

ALP Action for Development through Libraries Programme. An IFLA program to further the library profession, library institutions and library and information services in developing countries
http://www.ifla.org/VI/1/alp.htm

alphabetic designation Numbering system for serials using letters rather than numbers—e.g., Part A, Part B, Part C

alphanumeric Containing, or likely to contain, both letters and numbers

alternative title The second part of a title proper consisting of two parts; the parts are joined by the word 'or'—e.g., *As You Like It, or, What You Will*

amendment A correction or improvement

Americana Material relating to American history, geography, or folklore

American Association of Law Libraries AALL. Organization of law librarians and related professionals, founded to develop law libraries and librarianship
http://www.aallnet.org/

American Indian Library Association AILA. A group founded to address the library-related needs of American Indians and Alaska Natives
http://ailanet.org/

American Library Association ALA. U.S. professional library organization that aims to support and promote libraries and the library profession. See their website for their divisions, publications, awards and prizes
http://www.ala.org

American National Standards Institute ANSI. Disseminates basic standards like ASCII, and represents the U.S. at the International Organization for Standardization (ISO)
http://web.ansi.org

American Society for Indexing ASI. An organization of professional indexers, librarians, editors, publishers, and organizations that employ indexers, founded in 1968 to promote indexing, abstracting, and database building http://www.asindexing.org/

American Theological Library Association ATLA. An organization of professional theological librarians, people interested in theological librarianship, and theological institutions, founded in 1946 http://www.atla.com/

AMICUS 1. Free online union catalog of the holdings of 1300 Canadian libraries; includes *Canadiana*, the former print national bibliography of Library and Archives Canada. 2. Integrated library management software developed for and by the National Library of Canada http://www.collectionscanada.ca/amicus/

amnesty Waiving library fines in exchange for the return of overdue books

analects Parts of a literary work or group of works, literary gleanings

analytical description In RDA, a bibliographic description for a part of a larger resource (e.g., a single volume of a three-volume biography, a single map forming part of a map series). Cf comprehensive description, hierarchical description

analytical entry In AACR2, an entry for part of a resource (e.g., a chapter in a book, book in series, song on a CD) for which a comprehensive catalog record is also made. RDA uses the term 'analytical description' for this concept

analytical title added entry In AACR2, a title added entry for part of a work

analytical title page The title page of an individual monograph that is part of a series, used in AACR2 cataloging as a title page substitute when there is no series title page

ANBD Australian National Bibliographic Database. Bibliographic records from national cataloging agencies in Australia, Britain, Canada, New Zealand, Singapore and the United States; and from libraries that contribute records to Libraries Australia and NZNB, including holdings http://www.nla.gov.au/librariesaustralia/about/anbd/

android An operating system designed for touchscreen mobile devices such as smartphones and tablet computers. Cf iOS

Anglo-American Cataloguing Rules Second edition, Second edition 2002 revision AACR2, AACR2R. A set of rules for descriptive cataloging adopted by libraries in English-speaking countries. Replaced by RDA (*Resource Description and Access*) in 2010

annals The formal record of the proceedings of an organization or an academic society, or events and developments in a specific discipline or field of study

annotated bibliography A bibliography with comments on each item

annotation A note of explanation or comment

annual (adj) Published once a year. (n) A serial published once a year

annual report An official publication reviewing the activities of an organization for one year

annual review A publication that reviews the literature or current research on a topic for a year

anonymous Of unknown authorship

ANSI American National Standards Institute. Disseminates basic standards like ASCII, and represents the U.S. at the International Organization for Standardization (ISO)
http://web.ansi.org

anthology A collection of works or extracts of works by different authors

antiquarian bookseller A bookseller who deals in old and rare books

ANZSI Australian and New Zealand Society of Indexers Inc. Aims to represent the interests of indexers and to provide training and other resources to Australians and New Zealanders involved in indexing
http://www.anzsi.org/site/

APA–FT Australian Public Affairs–Full Text. An online collection of scanned images of articles from more than 500 Australian journals indexed in APAIS, the Australian Public Affairs Information Service
http://www.informit.com.au/products/ProductDetails.aspx?container=apaft
https://www.nla.gov.au/apais/

APAIS Australian Public Affairs Information Service. Subject and author index to current Australian literature on current affairs, economics, humanities, law, literature, politics and social sciences, produced by the National Library of Australia. Available online from Informit. Cf APA–FT
http://www.informit.com.au/products/indexes.aspx?id=APAIS
https://www.nla.gov.au/apais/

APALA Asian Pacific American Librarians Association. An organization founded to address the information needs of Asian/Pacific American communities
http://www.apalaweb.org/

APA style A bibliographic format for citing information based on the requirements of the American Psychological Association. Cf electronic style, MLA style, Chicago style, Harvard style
http://www.apastyle.org/

aperture card A card with one or more pieces of microfilm inserted in it

APIN Asia Pacific Information Network. A network formed by UNESCO in 2002 as an information hub to promote information accessibility, information literacy and sharing of information resources in Southeast, South and Central Asia and the Pacific
http://www.unescobkk.org/communication-and-information/knowledge-societies/apin/

apocryphal Of doubtful authorship or authenticity

app (Plural apps) A self-contained program or piece of software designed to fulfil a particular purpose. Apps can run on the Internet, on a computer, on a phone or on other electronic devices. Cf applet, mobile app

appendix (Plural appendices) Additional material such as statistics, tables etc. attached as a separate item at the end of a work

applet A small, often free, computer program (i.e., 'application') that performs a simple task. Cf app, mobile app

application service provider ASP. A company that leases computer software or provides Internet hosting to users

approval plan Also on-approval plan. A library's instruction to a publisher or supplier to provide one copy of all publications in a particular category, with the right to return them. Cf blanket order

APRA Australasian Performing Rights Association. The organization that grants licenses to broadcast or perform musical works in public on behalf of the owners of copyright in musical works
http://www.apra.com.au

Aquabrowser Discovery layer software from Proquest. Cf discovery layer

arabic numeral A number like 1, 2, 3...

ARANZ Archives and Records Association of New Zealand. An organization concerned with New Zealand records and information management
http://www.aranz.org.nz/

archival resource In RDA, records or documents created and/or used by a person, family or corporate body and preserved for their continuing value. The resource may be a collection, aggregation of documents or a discrete item

archive 1. A body of historical records of an organization. 2. Collection of computer files related to a subject, stored on a computer, disc or tape

archives 1. Records or historical documents preserved permanently because of their enduring value. 2. The storage area where archival material is kept. 3. An organization responsible for the care and control of archival material

Archives and Records Association of New Zealand ARANZ. An organization concerned with New Zealand records and information management
http://www.aranz.org.nz/

Archives nationales du Québec. *See* Bibliothèque et Archives nationales du Québec (BAnQ)

Archives New Zealand / Te Rua Mahara o te Kawanatanga The organization that ensures access to and preservation of New Zealand government records
http://www.archives.govt.nz/

archivist A person who collects and preserves archival material

area of description In an AACR2 cataloging record created using the International Standard Bibliographic Description (ISBD), an area of description constitutes a major section of the bibliographic description, dealing with a particular category—e.g., publication details. ISBD nominates nine areas of description. Cf ISBD

Ariel Software that enables users to scan articles and images, and transmit the resulting image over the Internet to other Ariel workstations, an email address or a web server
http://www.infotrieve.com/ariel-interlibrary-loan-software

ARL Association of Research Libraries. An organization founded in 1932 comprising the libraries of North American research institutions, that operates as a forum for the exchange of ideas and as an agent for collective action
http://www.arl.org/

ARLIS/ANZ Art Libraries Society—Australia and New Zealand. An organization that fosters excellence in arts librarianship and visual resources curatorship
http://www.arlis.org.au/

ARLIS/NA Art Libraries Society of North America. An organization of art librarians founded in 1972 to foster excellence in art and design librarianship and image management
http://www.arlisna.org/

article A contribution to a serial written by one or more authors

artifact, artefact An object made by a person

Art Libraries Society—Australia and New Zealand ARLIS/ANZ. An organization that fosters excellence in arts librarianship and visual resources curatorship
http://www.arlis.org.au/

Art Libraries Society of North America ARLIS/NA. An organization of art librarians founded in 1972 to foster excellence in art and design librarianship and image management
http://www.arlisna.org/

art library A library that specializes in information and resources on the visual arts (drawing, painting, sculpture, graphic design, etc.)

ASA Australian Society of Archivists. The professional organization that represents archivists in Australia, founded in 1975
http://www.archivists.org.au

ASCII American Standard Code for Information Interchange. The de facto world standard for converting data into digital code to store in a computer. Cf Unicode

ASI American Society for Indexing. An organization of professional indexers, librarians, editors, publishers, and organizations that employ indexers, founded in 1968 to promote indexing, abstracting, and database building
http://www.asindexing.org/

Asian Pacific American Librarians Association APALA. An organization founded to address the information needs of Asian/Pacific American communities
http://www.apalaweb.org/

Asia Pacific Information Network APIN. A network formed by UNESCO in 2002 as an information hub to promote information accessibility, information literacy and sharing of information resources in Southeast, South and Central Asia and the Pacific
http://www.unescobkk.org/communication-and-information/knowledge-societies/apin/

ask a librarian services Also digital reference services, virtual reference services. Reference assistance by library professionals, given online to library clients who may email, post questions, submit reference forms or engage in interactive chats or instant messaging

ASLA Australian School Library Association. An independent federation of Australian State and Territory associations of teacher-librarians
http://www.asla.org.au/

ASLIB Association for Information Management. An independent international organization to help people who are not necessarily librarians manage information and knowledge in organizations, through training, advice, networking and continuing professional development
http://www.aslib.co.uk

ASP 1. application service provider. A company that leases computer software or provides Internet hosting to users. 2. File suffix ('.asp') for web pages created on the fly from web databases

Association Canadienne des Bibliothèques de Droit / Canadian Association of Law Libraries ACBD/CALL. An association that promotes law libraries and professional development in law librarianship in Canada
http://www.callacbd.ca/

association copy A book that has a special association with its author, another notable person, or a particular library or collection

Association des Archivistes du Québec AAQ. An association that promotes services and professional development in French to Quebec archivists
http://www.archivistes.qc.ca/

Association des Cartothèques et Archives Cartographiques du Canada / Association of Canadian Map Libraries and Archives ACACC/ACMLA. The professional organization for Canadian map librarians, cartographic archivists, and geographic information specialists
http://www.acmla.org/

Association for Library and Information Science Education ALISE. A U.S. organization founded in 1915, that promotes excellence in research, teaching, and service for library and information science education
http://www.alise.org/

Association for Information Management ASLIB. An independent international organization to help people who are not necessarily librarians manage information and knowledge in organizations, through training, advice, networking and continuing professional development
http://www.aslib.co.uk

Association of Canadian Archivists ACA. An association founded in 1975, devoted to professional and research activities of Canadian archivists
http://archivists.ca/

Association of Canadian Map Libraries and Archives / Association des Cartothèques et Archives Cartographiques du Canada ACMLA/ACACC. The professional organization for Canadian map librarians, cartographic archivists, and geographic information specialists
http://www.acmla.org/

Association of Commonwealth Archivists and Records Managers ACARM. An organization that promotes the development of professional archival and records management standards in the British Commonwealth
http://www.acarm.org/

Association of European Research Libraries / Ligue des Bibliothèques Européennes de Recherche LIBER. The principal association of the major research libraries of Europe, founded under the auspices of the Council of Europe
http://libereurope.eu/

Association of Jewish Libraries An organization that promotes Jewish literacy through enhancement of libraries and library resources and through leadership for the profession and practitioners of Judaica librarianship
http://www.jewishlibraries.org/

Association of Research Libraries ARL. An organization founded in 1932 comprising the libraries of North American research institutions, that operates as a forum for the exchange of ideas and as an agent for collective action
http://www.arl.org/

ATLA American Theological Library Association. An organization of professional theological librarians, people interested in theological librarianship, and theological institutions, founded in 1946
http://www.atla.com/

atlas A volume of maps or charts with or without explanations

ATSILIRN Aboriginal & Torres Strait Islander Library, Information and Resource Network Inc. Established in 1993 to support Australian Aboriginal and Torres Strait Islander library and information workers, and to improve the way information professionals perceive the information needs of Aboriginal and Torres Strait Islander peoples
http://aiatsis.gov.au/atsilirn/index.php

attribute In RDA, a property or identifying characteristic of an entity, used to describe entities. Attributes can include title, language, medium of performance, intended audience, date, physical format, edition, provenance, condition, etc. for library materials; and titles, gender, occupation, address, field of activity etc. for people, families or corporate bodies

audiobook Also book-on-tape, talking book. A book that has been read onto audiotape, CD or mp3 player

audiocassette Audiotape in plastic housing

audiotape Strip of mylar plastic tape covered with iron oxide that can be magnetized. Sound is encoded as magnetic signals

audiovisual AV. Can be heard and/or seen. Used for non-print

audiovisual equipment, audiovisual hardware Equipment used to access the information stored on audiovisual software

audiovisual material, audiovisual software Non-book materials like audiotapes, compact discs, slides, videotapes

audit trail A system that allows tracing of the detailed transactions underlying a record of financial or other activity

Aurora Foundation Ltd Established in 2001 to develop leadership capacity in the library and information management professions in Australia and New Zealand by developing and providing innovative and challenging programs
http://www.aurorafoundation.org.au

AUSMARC MARC format developed by the National Library of Australia. Replaced by MARC 21

AUSTLIT Australian Literary Database. Online database of Australian literature and literary criticism that aims to be the definitive research and information resource for Australian literary, print and narrative culture
http://www.austlit.edu.au/

Australasian Performing Rights Association APRA. The organization that grants licenses to broadcast or perform musical works in public on behalf of the owners of copyright in musical works
http://www.apra.com.au

Australian and New Zealand Society of Indexers Inc ANZSI. Aims to represent the interests of indexers and to provide training and other resources to Australians and New Zealanders involved in indexing
http://www.anzsi.org

Australian Archives *See* National Archives of Australia

Australian Books in Print *See* Global Books in Print

Australian Committee on Cataloguing ACOC. A joint committee of ALIA and the National Library charged with monitoring and influencing developments in national and international cataloging and classification
http://www.nla.gov.au/acoc

Australian Copyright Council ACC. An independent non-profit organization that aims to increase copyright awareness and influence changes to law and policy to benefit creators and copyright owners
http://www.copyright.org.au

Australian Council for Educational Research ACER. Independent educational research organization. Produces *Australian Education Index*
http://www.acer.edu.au

Australian Digital Theses Program A program to collect digitized copies of postgraduate theses produced at Australian universities, and make them accessible via the Web. Incorporated into Trove in 2011

Australian Government Index to Publications *See* GovPubs

Australian Government Libraries Information Network AGLIN. A network of librarians in Australian government libraries, who aim to represent the interests of member libraries and information services, and to develop and implement cooperative schemes and resources
http://www.aglin.org/

Australian Government Locator Service AGLS. A set of metadata elements based on the Dublin Core Element Set, with minor variations to suit Australian Government requirements, used to describe Internet resources
http://www.agls.gov.au/

Australian Government Publications Guide GovPubs. A guide to selected types of Australian government publications, such as acts, Hansards, gazettes and parliamentary papers, that are located in Australia's national, state and territory libraries or available on the Internet. The database is still searchable but no longer maintained
http://www.nla.gov.au/govpubs/

Australian Governments Interactive Functions Thesaurus AGIFT. A thesaurus that describes the business functions carried out across Commonwealth, State and local governments in Australia
http://agift.naa.gov.au

Australian Interlibrary Resource Sharing Code ILRS Code. A code of practice for interlibrary loan/document delivery that outlines agreed principles and service level standards
https://www.alia.org.au/resources-and-information/interlibrary-lending/australian-interlibrary-resource-sharing-ilrs-code

Australian Interlibrary Resource Sharing Directory ILRS Directory. A directory published by the National Library of Australia to assist libraries in interlibrary lending, containing National Union Catalogue (NUC) symbols and details of participating libraries, including contact details, charges, library policies etc.
http://www.nla.gov.au/ilrs

Australian Joint Copying Project A project that copied British archival material for the use of Australian and New Zealand historical researchers between 1948 and 1993. Available on microfilm at the National Library of Australia
http://www.nla.gov.au/collect/ajcp.html

Australian Libraries Copyright Committee ALCC. A policy body for the discussion of copyright issues affecting the library, archive and information sectors. It advocates for copyright law reform on behalf of libraries and copyright users
http://libcopyright.org.au/

Australian Libraries Gateway A website hosted by the National Library of Australia that provides access to libraries and other sources of information
http://www.nla.gov.au/libraries

Australian Libraries: The Essential Directory ALED. National printed directory of Australian academic, public, joint use and special libraries; and other information relevant to the library and information industry—e.g., associations, library suppliers etc.

Australian Library and Information Association ALIA. The professional association of Australian librarians, library technicians and organizations, whose aim is to support and promote libraries in the community. See their website for their interest groups, publications, awards and prizes
http://www.alia.org.au

Australian Library and Information Week Begun in 1968, and celebrated in May each year to showcase libraries and information agencies and their professional staff, and to introduce new services and skills to the community

Australian Literary Database AUSTLIT. Online database of Australian literature and literary criticism that aims to be the definitive research and information resource for Australian literary, print and narrative culture
http://www.austlit.edu.au/

Australian National Bibliographic Database ANBD. A database of bibliographic records from national cataloging agencies in Australia, Britain, Canada, New Zealand, Singapore and the United States; and from libraries that contribute records to Libraries Australia and NZNB, including holdings
http://www.nla.gov.au/librariesaustralia/about/anbd/

Australian Public Affairs–Full Text APA–FT. An online collection of scanned images of articles from more than 500 Australian journals indexed in APAIS, the Australian Public Affairs Information Service
http://www.informit.com.au/products/ProductDetails.aspx?container=apaft
https://www.nla.gov.au/apais/

Australian Public Affairs Information Service APAIS. Subject and author index to current Australian literature on current affairs, economics, humanities, law, literature, politics and social sciences, produced by the National Library of Australia. Available online from Informit
http://www.informit.com.au/products/indexes.aspx?id=APAIS
https://www.nla.gov.au/apais/

Australian School Library Association ASLA. An independent federation of Australian state and territory associations of teacher-librarians
http://www.asla.org.au/

Australian Society of Archivists ASA. The professional organization that represents archivists in Australia, founded in 1975
http://www.archivists.org.au

Australian Subject Access Project A project of the National Library of Australia that aims to maximize online access to Australian subject terms by adding SLASH terms to the Australian National Bibliographic Database while they are still awaiting approval by the Library of Congress. Cf SLASH
https://www.nla.gov.au/librariesaustralia/about/expert-advisory-groups/subject-headings-review-panel/australian-subject-access-project/

Australia's Research and Education Network AARNet. An electronic network of regional networks providing access to the Internet and electronic sharing of information to Australian universities and research agencies
http://www.aarnet.edu.au/

AUSTROM A CD-ROM and online collection of major Australian indexing and abstracting services
http://www.informit.com.au/indexes_AUSTROM_OL.html

authentication 1. Determining that a document or its reproduction is what it appears or purports to be. 2. A security procedure for checking a network user's identity and authorization

author Also personal author. 1. In AACR2, The person chiefly responsible for the intellectual or artistic content of a work. 2. Author: in RDA, a person, family or corporate body responsible for creating a work that is primarily textual in content, regardless of media type (e.g., printed, electronic or tactile text or spoken word) or of genre (e.g., poems, screenplays, blogs). Cf creator

authoring The use of special (authoring) tools to construct a multimedia application

authorised access point *See* authorized access point

authority control The control of access points by establishing and using consistent headings

authority file A collection of authority records containing the preferred forms of headings for names, series and subjects. It can be on cards, fiche or online

authority record A record of the preferred heading for a person, place, corporate body, series or title, giving information about the preferred heading and non-preferred alternatives, as well as notes about how these were derived

authority work The establishment and maintenance of authority files

authorization code Also access code. A username and/or password that is entered by a user to gain access to a computer system, network, or database (e.g., student access to a university computer network)

authorized access point In RDA, the preferred title or name to be used as an access point in a descriptive cataloging record. Cf variant access point

authorized access point for related entity The RDA term for the concept known in AACR2 cataloging as a 'see also reference', it provides a direction from one heading to another when both are used in cataloging

author number *See* book number

authorship Having some (or all) intellectual responsibility for creating a work

author statement In AACR2, the part of the description of a resource indicating intellectual and/or artistic responsibility

autobiography The story of a person's life written by him/herself

automated library management system ALMS. Also ILS, ILMS. An automated package of library services that contains several functions such as circulation, cataloging etc.

automatic abstracting Automatic production of an abstract, without human effort, based on a document's keywords and phrases

automatic indexing Indexing without human input, whereby the computer selects terms to represent a document using algorithms and software

autonym A work published under an author's own name. Cf allonym, pseudonym

auxiliary table A table of numbers and/or letters that can be added to notation in the schedules to make a classification number more specific

back file Non-current issues of a periodical, usually bound in annual volumes or converted to another format

back issue A non-current issue of a serial

backlist Non-current publications that a publisher or bookseller keeps in stock to meet future requests

backlog A quantity of library tasks—e.g., cataloging, fallen behind schedule

back matter Also end matter. The material at the end of a work, following the text—e.g., appendices, index

back order An order that could not be completed when placed, and which is held open for future delivery

back run A complete sequence of non-current issues of a serial

back set A set of non-current issues of a serial

Banned Books Week A week of activity celebrated annually in the U.S. since 1982, that draws attention to books whose availability is suppressed, or whose suppression had been attempted, because their content is considered objectionable or dangerous

banner 1. The strip of information on the front page of a newspaper that contains editorial and publishing details. 2. A narrow strip of advertising or identification of ownership displayed on a web page

banning Forbidding client privileges such as borrowing, usually until fines are paid

BAnQ Bibliothèque et Archives nationales du Québec. Provincial body founded to preserve records of Quebec's history from the seventeenth century onwards
http://www.banq.qc.ca

barcode Product identification code that can be read by an electronic barcode scanner. Used to identify, order, sell and manage library items using automated systems

barcode reader, barcode scanner A device used to read a barcode into a computer

base number The number found in the schedules of a classification scheme to which a number can be added from the tables

bastard title Also fly-title, half title. The brief title of a book that appears on the leaf preceding the title page

batch loading Loading groups of cataloging records to a larger database (e.g., WorldCat or Libraries Australia) from a local system, usually not in real time. Cf upline loading

batch processing Procedure by which data are collected by the computer and processed together, usually at a time when there is less demand on computing resources (e.g., overnight). Cf real-time processing

Bath Profile An international Z39.50 specification that supports library applications and resource discovery; until recently, maintained by the Library and Archives of Canada

bay 1. A set of library shelves between two uprights. 2. A U-shaped arrangement of shelves

belles-lettres Writings of a purely literary kind

benchmark Level of achievement in an activity or organization, or by a person, against which quality of performance is assessed

BERITA A bibliographic database that indexes articles about Brunei, Malaysia, Singapore and South-East Asia, available online from Informit
http://www.informit.com.au/products/indexes.aspx?id=BERITA

Berne Convention An international convention originally signed in 1886, since revised several times, that provides reciprocal protection of copyright in the member countries
http://www.wipo.int/treaties/en/ip/berne/

Beta Phi Mu Library and information studies international honor society
http://beta-phi-mu.org/

beta test, beta testing A test of new or revised hardware or software carried out by users under normal operating conditions

bi-annual Issued twice a year

BIBCO Bibliographic record component of the Program for Cooperative Cataloging of the Library of Congress
http://www.loc.gov/aba/pcc/bibco

BIBFRAME Bibliographic Framework Initiative. A proposed new bibliographic framework that will serve as an encoding standard for RDA and replace MARC, based on link data principles. Being developed under the auspices of the Library of Congress, still in very early stages
http://www.loc.gov/bibframe/

bibliographer A person who prepares bibliographies

bibliographic Related to books or other library materials

Bibliographical Society of Canada / La Société bibliographique du Canada BSC/SBC. A society that promotes bibliographical activity and research
http://www.bsc-sbc.ca/

Bibliographic Classification Also Bliss Classification. A classification scheme devised by H. E. Bliss, using letters and numbers. Completely revised in 1976, but not widely used

bibliographic control The creation, organization, and management of records to describe resources held in libraries or databases, and to facilitate user access

bibliographic database A computerized file of electronic records, each of which represents a bibliographic item that can be retrieved by author, title, subject heading, or keywords

bibliographic description Description of a resource by title, statement of responsibility, edition, date, publishing information etc.

Bibliographic Framework Initiative BIBFRAME. A proposed new bibliographic framework that will serve as an encoding standard for RDA and replace MARC, based on linked data principles. Being developed under the auspices of the Library of Congress, still in very early stages http://www.loc.gov/bibframe/

bibliographic ghost Also ghost. A work or edition of a work recorded in bibliographies, catalogs, and other sources, that may not exist

bibliographic identity A name under which a person writes a particular kind of material

bibliographic instruction Also client education, library orientation, reader education, reader instruction, user education. Helping people to derive the most benefit from using a library

bibliographic item Also bibliographic resource. A document or set of documents in any physical format that has been published or treated as a single entity

bibliographic level 1. In AACR2, the complexity of bibliographic description of a resource being cataloged. 2. Byte 7 of the MARC leader. The most common values are '**m**' for monograph and '**s**' for serial

bibliographic record Also catalog record, catalogue record. A description of a resource in card, microtext, machine-readable or other form containing sufficient information to identify the resource. It describes the intellectual and physical characteristics of the resource. It may include subject headings and call number

bibliographic resource Also bibliographic item. A document or documents in any physical format that has been published or treated as a single entity

bibliographic retrieval Querying a database of library holdings or published documents, and retrieving relevant information

bibliographic tools Resources used to provide information about and access to books and other material

bibliography A list of materials or resources, usually either subject-related or on the works of one author

bibliometrics 1. The use of statistics to analyze the use of a library's materials and services. 2. Measuring developments in a discipline by analyzing books and journal articles in that field

bibliophile A person who loves books, especially in physical form

Bibliothèque et Archives Canada / Library and Archives Canada LAC. The national organization established in 2004 combining the holdings, services and staff of the former National Library of Canada and National Archives of Canada
http://www.bac-lac.gc.ca/

Bibliothèque et Archives nationales du Québec BAnQ. Provincial body founded to preserve records of Quebec's history from the seventeenth century onwards
http://www.banq.qc.ca/

Bibliothèque nationale de France BnF. The national library of France
http://www.bnf.fr/

Bibliothèque scientifique nationale / National Science Library The library of the National Research Council Canada, providing information and services to support Canadian discovery, innovation and commercialization activities
http://www.nrc-cnrc.gc.ca/eng/publications/library/

biennial Issued every two years. Cf semiannual

bimonthly 1. Issued every two months. 2. Issued twice a month. Cf semimonthly

binder's title The title lettered on the spine of a book when it is re-bound

bindery A workshop where books and serials are bound

binding 1. The type of cover of a book—usually called hardback or paperback, but sometimes cased, hard bound, hard cover (hardback) or limp, softback (paperback). 2. Adding a hard cover to a book or volume of serials

binding record A list of books sent to the binder

binding slip The form on which instructions for binding are written

biographical dictionary, biographical directory A listing of people, usually in alphabetical order of surname, providing details of dates, titles, birthplace, family etc.

biography 1. A written account of a person's life. 2. The branch of literature concerned with people's individual lives

BIP Books in Print. Also Global Books in Print. Listing of over 20 million in-print, out-of-print, and forthcoming book, audio, and video titles, available online, on CD-ROM and in print. Available in U.S. edition or Global Edition http://www.booksinprint.com/ or http://www.bowker.com

biweekly 1. Issued every two weeks. 2. Issued twice a week. Cf semiweekly

BL British Library. The national library of the United Kingdom http://www.bl.uk

blanket order An instruction to a publisher or supplier to provide one copy of all publications in a particular category, without the right to return them. Cf approval plan

blind reference A cross-reference in an index or catalog, directing the reader to a heading that does not exist

Bliss Classification Also Bibliographic Classification. A classification scheme devised by H. E. Bliss, using letters and numbers. Completely revised in 1976, but not widely used

blue book 1. An official list of people in the employ of the U.S. government. 2. An official government report bound in a blue cover, especially one published by the British or Canadian government. 3. Also state manual. A government manual that lists government agencies and structures, voting districts, etc. 4. A blank notebook with blue covers used to write examination answers

BLUEcloud Suite An integrated library management system developed by SirsiDynix for use in conjunction with its Horizon or Symphony products, augmenting these systems with cloud-based discovery components http://www.sirsidynix.com/bluecloud-suite

blurb Also puff (American usage). Description of a book by the publisher, usually found on the back cover or book jacket, or in an advertising brochure or catalog

BNB British National Bibliography. A listing of new British publications received by the Legal Deposit Office of the British Library and other British legal deposit libraries, including full cataloging data. Available electronically http://www.bl.uk/bibliographic/natbib.html

BnF Bibliothèque nationale de France. The national library of France
http://www.bnf.fr/

board book A book for very young children made of cardboard pages with illustrations and very little or no text

boards Pieces of strong card etc. used for the hard cover of a book

Bodleian Library The main reference library of Oxford University in England
http://www.bodleian.ox.ac.uk/bodley

book band A strip of paper around the cover of a book that highlights a special characteristic—e.g., 3-day loan

book bin A box on wheels into which books and other library materials are returned

book box scheme Provision of books in boxes for users who do not have access, or to supplement limited access, to a library

book card A piece of card or plastic that has details of a particular book—e.g., author, title, call number. Used when manually charging out a loan

book catalog, book catalogue 1. A catalog printed and bound in book format. 2. A substantial list of book titles distributed by a publisher or bookseller

book club 1. A company that sells new books by mail to subscribers who buy a minimum number of titles each year. 2. *See* reading group

book collection Also book stock. All the items in a library's book collection

book cradle A wooden, metal or plastic stand in which an open book is displayed

bookcrossing The practice of leaving a book in a public place to be picked up and read by others, who then do likewise
http://www.bookcrossing.com/

book drop Also book return. A chute or box into which books and other library materials are returned, especially when a library is closed

bookend Also book support. An 'L' or 'T' shaped piece of steel, wood or plastic placed at the end of a row of books to keep them upright

Booker Prize *See* Man Booker Prize for Fiction

book exchange A place where reading material is exchanged, often with payment

book jacket Also dust cover, dust jacket, dust wrapper, jacket, wrapper. Paper cover for a hard-bound book

book jobber Also jobber. A wholesale bookseller who supplies books to retailers and libraries. Cf library supplier

booklet Also pamphlet. A small (usually less than fifty pages) printed work on a topic of current interest

book lift A mechanical device for transporting books from one floor to another in a library

bookmarking 1. Marking a place in a book. 2. Making a link to an Internet site so that you can return directly to it later

bookmobile A van containing library materials that travels to different locations to provide a library service

book number The numbers, letters or combination of numbers and letters used to distinguish an individual item from other items with the same classification number. Cf Cutter number

book-on-tape Also audiobook, talking book. A book that has been read onto audiotape, CD or mp3 player

book plate A small label showing the book's owner, pasted inside a book

book return Also book drop. A chute or box into which books and other library materials are returned, especially when a library is closed

book review Description and evaluation of a book in terms of its purpose and intended audience

books-by-mail Circulation of library materials by mail, usually to rural and housebound populations

book scout A person who searches for rare or hard-to-find books on request

bookseller A person who sells books at retail prices, especially via a bookstore

Books in Print BIP. Also Global Books in Print. Listing of over 20 million in-print, out-of-print, and forthcoming book, audio, and video titles, available online, on CD-ROM and in print. Available in U.S. edition or Global Edition http://www.booksinprint.com/   or   http://www.bowker.com

bookstacks Also stacks 1. The rows of shelves containing a library's collection. 2. An area containing seldom-used library materials, usually accessible only to library staff

book stamp An inked impression stamped onto the cover, title or end paper of a book, signalling its owner

book stock Also book collection. All the items in a library's book collection

book support Also bookend. An 'L' or 'T' shaped piece of steel, wood or plastic placed at the end of a row of books to keep them upright

book trade journal A periodical issued by publishers, booksellers, and others in the book trade to announce and promote new items

book truck Also reshelving cart. A wheeled trolley used for returning books to their shelves or other areas in the library

bookworm 1. The larva of a moth or beetle that burrows into the covers and pages of books. Cf silverfish. 2. A person who reads voraciously

Boolean logic Use of the terms 'and', 'or', 'not' to formulate online search commands, to represent any logical possibility

Boolean operator A particular word used in formulating a search strategy to retrieve online information: **And**: retrieves only items with both terms; **Or**: retrieves items with either term; **Not**: retrieves items with one term and not the other. Cf tilde

Boolean searching Searching a database or document using Boolean operators (and, or, not) to specify and limit the search

born digital material Resources created in electronic format, as opposed to print material that was subsequently converted to digital form

borrower A member of a lending library

borrower's card Also library card. A paper or plastic card that shows a registered borrower is entitled to check out materials from a library

borrowing period Also checkout period, loan period. The time for which an item in a library may be checked out by a borrower

braille Embossed print using raised dots to represent the letters of the alphabet, enabling visually impaired people to read by touch

branch library A library other than the central library in a system

British Library BL. The national library of the United Kingdom
http://www.bl.uk

British National Bibliography BNB. A listing of new British publications received by the Legal Deposit Office of the British Library and other British legal deposit libraries, including full cataloging data. Available electronically
http://www.bl.uk/bibliographic/natbib.html

broad classification Classification using the main divisions and subdivisions of a scheme without breaking down into narrower concepts. Cf close classification

broader term BT. A more general subject heading. Cf narrower term, related term

broadsheet, broadside A large sheet of paper usually printed on one side

Broad System of Ordering BSO. A machine-held classification system embracing all fields of knowledge
http://www.ucl.ac.uk/fatks/bso/

brochure A publication consisting of one or a few leaves of printed material

broken link A link on a website that no longer connects to another site

Browne loan system A manual circulation system using a book card and a borrower pocket. The book card is filed in the borrower's pocket in date due order

browse 1. To examine a collection of library materials in an unsystematic way. 2. To look through a list of names, subjects, etc., rather than going straight to a particular term

browser A computer program used to view and interact with the Internet, web servers in private networks, or files in file systems. Cf web browser

BSC/SBC Bibliographical Society of Canada / La Société bibliographique du Canada. A society that promotes bibliographical activity and research
http://www.bsc-sbc.ca/

BSO Broad System of Ordering. A machine-held classification system embracing all fields of knowledge
http://www.ucl.ac.uk/fatks/bso/

BT Broader term. A more general subject heading. Cf NT, RT

buckram Coarse cotton cloth sized with glue, used in binding to cover and protect heavily used books

bulk lending Lending a large volume of material from one library to another library, school, community centre, etc.

bulk order An instruction to a publisher or supplier to provide a certain quantity of a particular type of resource—e.g., popular fiction

bulletin A publication of an organization (including libraries) containing information for members and/or users

bulletin board A notice board in a library or online, displaying information about new acquisitions, coming events etc.

byline In a newspaper or magazine, a statement of the authorship of an article

byte The basic unit of computer storage; it holds the equivalent of a single character—e.g., a letter, number, dollar sign

CAB current awareness bulletin. A publication provided by a library to keep users up-to-date with information in their interest areas

CAL Copyright Agency Limited. The organization that represents Australian authors, artists and publishers in collecting photocopying and rights licensing fees
http://www.copyright.com.au

Caldecott Medal An annual award made by the American Library Association to the illustrator of the most distinguished children's picture book
http://www.ala.org/alsc/awardsgrants/bookmedia/caldecottmedal/caldecottmedal

calendar 1. A list of the days in a year, sometimes indicating holidays or other significant days. 2. Archives: A chronological annotated list of the documents in a collection. 3. Paper manufacture: 'calendared' paper is a heavy glossy paper often used for artwork reproductions or photographs in books

Calibre A free open source application that converts text, HTML and other files into a range of e-book formats, and includes library management components to sort and search library e-books by various categories
http://calibre-ebook.com/

CALL/ACBD Canadian Association of Law Libraries / Association Canadienne des Bibliothèques de Droit. An association that promotes law libraries and professional development in law librarianship in Canada
http://www.callacbd.ca/

call number A number on a library item consisting of a classification number, a book number and often a location symbol

call slip A form to be filled out by a borrower to request an item from the closed stacks of a library

Canada.ca The official website of the federal government of Canada, merging over 1500 individual websites for departments and agencies into one portal that provides access to government departments, services and information
http://www.canada.ca/

Canadiana The national bibliography of Canada, subsumed into AMICUS.

Canadian Association of Law Libraries / Association Canadienne des Bibliothèques de Droit CALL/ACBD. An association that promotes law libraries and professional development in law librarianship in Canada
http://www.callacbd.ca/

Canadian Business and Current Affairs CBCA. A suite of online databases providing indexing, abstracts and full-text articles on Canadian business, current events, education and reference topics. Available by subscription through Proquest Dialog
http://www.proquest.com/libraries/academic/databases/cbca.html

Canadian Heritage Information Network / Réseau canadien d'information sur le patrimoine CHIN/RCIP. A network of Canadian museums and heritage organizations that aims to promote the development, presentation and preservation of Canada's digital heritage
http://www.chin.gc.ca/

Canadian Library Association CLA. Professional English language library association that represents the interests of librarianship in Canada. See their website for their committees, networks, publications and awards http://www.cla.ca

Canadian Library Month The month of October, designated by the Canadian Library Association as a time to raise public awareness of the valuable role that libraries play in the lives of Canadians

Canadian Newsstand A full-text online database of Canadian newspapers with coverage from 1977, available by subscription through Proquest Dialog http://www.proquest.com/products-services/canadian_newsstand.html

Canadian Research Knowledge Network CRKN. A partnership of Canadian universities, dedicated to expanding access to scholarly research in digital formats. It builds on the Canadian National Site Licensing Project, under which over 2,200 journals and research databases were made available online http://crkn.ca/

CANARIE A government-supported organization established to advance Canada's Internet infrastructure, that has developed and delivered the high-speed, high capacity fibre optic CANARIE network for Canada's research and education communities http://www.canarie.ca/

Canberra Qualifiers A set of terms—type, scheme, and language—designed to qualify the Dublin Core Metadata Element Set, agreed to at the Canberra Metadata Workshop in 1997

CAN/MARC MARC format developed by the then National Library of Canada. Harmonized with USMARC to create MARC 21 in the late 1990s

caption A heading or title of a chapter, article or page

caption title A title given at the beginning of the first page of text

card catalog, card catalogue A catalog whose entries are on standard 3 x 5 inch (7.5 x 12.5 cm) cards and filed in drawers

Carnegie Medal An annual award made by the (British) Chartered Institute of Library and Information Professionals since 1936 to the writer of an outstanding children's book written in English http://www.carnegiegreenaway.org.uk/

carrel A desk with sides that provides some seclusion from other library users, and which can be reserved for one reader

carrier / carrier type In RDA, the packaging that houses a resource—e.g., audio disc, slide, volume, online resource, etc. Cf container, physical carrier

cartobibliography 1. An ordered list of citations to maps and/or works about maps. 2. The branch of bibliography dealing with maps and mapping

cartography The making of maps or charts

cartouche A frame or scroll in a corner of a map in which the title, cartographer, etc. are given

CAS Current awareness service. A service provided by a library to keep users up-to-date with information in their interest areas. Cf SDI

case A completed book cover ready to be fitted to form the cover of a book

case binding Bookbinding in which a hard cover (a case) is made separately, and then attached to the book. Cf paperback

cased Also hardback, hard bound, hard cover. Bound in cloth- or paper-covered boards. Cf paperback

case-sensitive Distinguishing between upper-case and lower-case letters

catalog, catalogue A list of library materials contained in a collection, a library or a group of libraries, arranged according to some definite plan

cataloger, cataloguer A person who prepares catalog entries and maintains a catalog so that library materials can be retrieved efficiently

cataloging, cataloguing The preparation of bibliographic information for catalog records; consists of descriptive cataloging, subject cataloging and classification

cataloging client, cataloguing client Software that enables a user to create cataloging records for a remote database (e.g., a national bibliographic database) and upload them

cataloging-in-publication, cataloguing in publication CIP. Cataloging data produced by the national library or other agency of the country of publication, included in the work when it is published

cataloging services, cataloguing services Services in or for a library that relate to the catalog; part of technical services

cataloging source, cataloguing source The agency that creates and/or modifies a MARC record

cataloging tools, cataloguing tools Publications of the international cataloging rules and standards, including *Resource Description and Access, Anglo-American Cataloguing Rules, Library of Congress Subject Headings, Library of Congress Classification, Dewey Decimal Classification*

catalog record, catalogue record Also bibliographic record. A description of a resource in card, microtext, machine-readable or other form containing sufficient information to identify the resource. It describes the intellectual and physical characteristics of the resource. It may include subject headings and call number

catch title Also catchword title. A partial title consisting of a memorable word or phrase likely to be used as a term in searching

catchword A word or part of a word printed prominently at the top of a page or column in a dictionary or encyclopedia, that repeats the first and last heading on the page or in the column

Catholic Library Association CLA. An international organization of librarians, teachers, and booksellers concerned with Catholic libraries and the writing, publishing, and distribution of Catholic literature, established in 1921
http://www.cathla.org/

CAUL Council of Australian University Librarians. The organization of librarians of all Australian universities, providing a forum for discussion of issues relating to libraries and a mechanism for the coordination of activities that benefit the university community
http://www.caul.edu.au/

CBC Children's Book Council. A non-profit trade association of U.S. children's book publishers, dedicated to informing the industry and fostering literacy. Sponsors of Children's Book Week
http://www.cbcbooks.org/

CBCA Canadian Business and Current Affairs. A suite of online databases providing indexing, abstracts and full-text articles on Canadian business, current events, education and reference topics. Available by subscription through Proquest Dialog
http://www.proquest.com/libraries/academic/databases/cbca.html

CCC Copyright Clearance Center. A U.S. organization providing collective copyright licenses to corporate and academic users of copyrighted materials
http://www.copyright.com/

CC:DA Committee on Cataloging: Description and Access. The body within the American Library Association responsible for developing official ALA positions on additions to and revisions of descriptive cataloging standards
http://www.ala.org/alcts/mgrps/camms/cmtes/ats-ccscat

CD Compact disc. A disc on which sound is recorded by a laser and covered with a protective coating. The disc is then played by a laser beam. Often used when referring to recorded music—e.g., 'music CD'

CDNL Conference of Directors of National Libraries. An international forum of directors of all national libraries
www.cdnl.info/

CDNLAO Conference of Directors of National Libraries of Asia and Oceania. An organization that aims to exchange information and promote cooperation for the development of libraries in Asia and Oceania
http://www.ndl.go.jp/en/cdnlao/index.html

CD-ROM Compact disc read-only memory. A computer disc on which data is recorded and read using a laser. CD-ROM discs provide large capacity storage for computer programs and data, including audio, video and graphics. Cf USB flash drive

censorship Prohibition against publishing or distributing material that is considered objectionable for social, political, religious or other reasons

centered heading A heading in Dewey Decimal Classification that applies to a range of classification numbers

Center for Research Libraries CRL. An international consortium of university, college and research libraries that acquires and preserves print and digital primary resource materials from at-risk areas and makes them available to member institutions through interlibrary loan and electronic delivery
http://www.crl.edu/

Center for the Book (USA) A partnership of the Library of Congress, collections in state libraries or major institutions, and private sector organizations, that aims to stimulate public interest in books, reading, libraries and literacy
http://www.read.gov/cfb

centralized cataloging, centralised cataloguing The cataloging of library materials for more than one library (branch etc.) carried out by a single central cataloging section

central library Also main library. The headquarters of a library system, where management decisions are made, and the main collection held

Centre for the Book (NZ) Established in 2011, the University of Otago Centre for the Book promotes the rich book heritage of the university, the city of Dunedin and the country of New Zealand, particularly its English and Maori resources
http://www.otago.ac.nz/books

Centre for the Book research unit (Australia) A part of Monash University, the unit charts book history and print culture in all forms, both historical and contemporary
http://artsonline.monash.edu.au/the-book/

Centre for the Book (South Africa) An outreach unit of the National Library of South Africa whose mission is easy access to books for all, and to promote a culture of reading, writing and publishing in local languages
http://www.nlsa.ac.za/index.php?option=com_content&view=article&id=53&Itemid=41

CERL Consortium of European Research Libraries. A group of European research libraries formed in 1992 to share resources and expertise with a view to improving access to and preservation of the European printed heritage
http://www.cerl.org/

cessation The termination of publication of a serial

chapter 1. A section of a book. 2. A branch of a society or organization

character set A group of symbols in a particular font, used for printing and/or electronic display

charging Recording the loan of an item

charging desk Also circulation desk, issue desk, loans desk. The area of the library where staff handle loans

chart 1. A map for navigation. 2. A poster containing factual information. 3. A diagram or graph

Chartered Institute of Library and Information Professionals CILIP. British professional body formed in 2002 from the merger of the Institute of Information Scientists (IIS) and The Library Association (LA)
http://www.cilip.org.uk/

check in To record the receipt of (usually a library item returned from loan)

check out To record the loan of (usually a library item being borrowed)

checkout period Also borrowing period, loan period. The time for which an item in a library may be checked out by a borrower

Chicago style A format for preparing research papers and citing references, developed by the University of Chicago Press. Cf APA style, MLA style, Harvard style

Chief Officers of State Library Agencies COSLA. An organization of the heads of U.S. state libraries, providing mechanisms for dealing with the issues faced by state librarians and directors responsible for statewide library development
http://www.cosla.org/

chief source of information In AACR2, this is the source from which a bibliographic description (or part of it) is prepared. RDA uses the term 'preferred sources of information'

Children's Book Council CBC. A non-profit trade association of U.S. children's book publishers, dedicated to informing the industry and fostering literacy. Sponsors of Children's Book Week
http://www.cbcbooks.org/

Children's Book Council of Australia A national organization with branches in each state and territory, whose main aim is to encourage children's enjoyment of books. It organizes Children's Book Week and publishes *Reading time*. See their website for their publications, awards and prizes
http://cbca.org.au/

Children's Literature Association of New Zealand. *See* Storylines Children's Literature Foundation and Storylines Trust

CHIN/RCIP Canadian Heritage Information Network / Réseau canadien d'information sur le patrimoine. A network of Canadian museums and heritage organizations that aims to promote the development, presentation and preservation of Canada's digital heritage
http://www.chin.gc.ca/

chronological designation Numbering of serials in the form of a date—e.g., January 2014. Cf numeric designation

chronology A list of events and their dates in the order of their occurrence, relevant to the topic of the book in which they appear

CIJE Current Index to Journals in Education. A U.S. index to education journals, published by ERIC, available through EBSCO

CILIP Chartered Institute of Library and Information Professionals. British professional body formed in 2002 from the merger of the Institute of Information Scientists (IIS) and The Library Association (LA)
http://www.cilip.org.uk/

CIP Cataloging-in-publication. Cataloging data produced by the national library or other agency of the country of publication, included in the work when it is published

circulating collection Books and other materials that may be borrowed by the library's clients

circulation Borrowing and returning of library items

circulation desk Also charging desk, issue desk, loans desk. The area of the library where staff handle loans

circulation list, circulation slip A list of users in an organization to whom a publication is to be sent, in the order decided by the library

circulation services All services concerned with lending materials—charging material in and out, retrieving, levying and collecting fines, etc.

circulation system A system that stores and matches information on a library item, a borrower and the date due

citation Reference to a text or part of a text from which a passage is quoted, or to a source regarded as an authority for a statement or argument

citation analysis Statistical analysis of the frequency with which particular sources are quoted

citation index 1. A list of articles that, after the appearance of the original article, refer to or cite that article. 2. A searchable database containing citations of journal articles

CJK Chinese Japanese Korean. Asian languages not using roman alphabets

CLA Canadian Library Association. Professional English language library association that represents the interests of librarianship in Canada. See their website for their committees, networks, publications and awards http://www.cla.ca

CLA Catholic Library Association. An international organization of librarians, teachers, and booksellers concerned with Catholic libraries and the writing, publishing, and distribution of Catholic literature, established in 1921 http://www.cathla.org/

CLA Copyright Licensing Agency. The British company that provides collective copyright licenses on behalf of authors, publishers and artists https://www.cla.co.uk/

claim A form or letter to a publisher or subscription agent notifying of a serial issue that has not been received

class The broadest grouping of numbers in a classification scheme representing a subject group or discipline—e.g., religion

classification A system for arranging library materials according to subject

classification number The number allocated to a resource to indicate its subject and group it with similar items

classification scheme A particular scheme for arranging library materials according to subject—e.g., *Dewey Decimal Classification, Library of Congress Classification*

classified catalog, classified catalogue A catalog in which the entries are arranged in order of classification number

classify To allocate a classification number

claw A device in a film projector that fits into the film sprocket holes and moves the film one frame at a time

clearinghouse An organization that collects, maintains and disseminates information about research, development and other activities and publications in a particular field

client 1. Also patron, user. A person who is served by an information agency. 2. In a network, a personal computer that requests information or applications from the network server

client education Also bibliographic instruction, library orientation, reader education, reader instruction, user education. Helping people to derive the most benefit from using the library

client/server A method of distributing information or files in which the main files and applications are kept on a central computer (server), and individuals request them via their own computer (client)

client services Also public services, reader services. Direct services to library users, including circulation, interlibrary loan, bibliographic instruction, and reference services. Cf reference services

client software Software that enables a user to seek information from a computer server, and receive it in a form compatible with the user's computer

clipping Also cutting. A page or pages cut out of a newspaper or some other printed material

clipping service A service that provides clients with news items from news services and other sources on a regular basis

CLIR Council on Library and Information Resources. An independent, non-profit organization based in the U.S. to enhance access to information in research, teaching and learning environments by working in collaboration with libraries, cultural institutions and communities of higher learning http://www.clir.org/

cloning, close cataloging, close cataloguing Also close copy cataloging. Creating a new cataloging record based on a record for a similar resource—e.g., the spoken word version of a monograph, or a new edition of the monograph—by copying the original record and making appropriate changes

close classification Classifying as specifically as possible, using all available subdivisions of a scheme. Cf broad classification

close copy cataloging, close copy cataloguing Also close cataloging, cloning. Creating a new cataloging record based on a record for a similar resource—e.g., the spoken word version of a monograph, or a new edition of the monograph—by copying the original record and making appropriate changes

closed access Where users only have access to items in the collection by requesting them from a member of the library staff. Most often occurs in large research libraries. Cf open access

closed entry A bibliographic record that contains complete information for all the parts or volumes of a serial. Cf open entry

closed file 1. A file of archived documents in which additions are not expected. 2. A file to which access is restricted or denied

closed reserve Also reserve collection, restricted loan, short loan. A collection of material in high demand, usually in a teaching institution, whose loan periods are shorter than normal library loans, housed in an area where only library staff have direct access to the material. Cf open reserve

closed stack An area containing under-used library materials, only accessible to library staff and sometimes a small group of special users. Often used interchangeably with 'closed access'

cloth book An illustrated book printed on strong cloth to resist rough treatment by very young children

cloud computing Storing and accessing data and programs over the Internet instead of via a computer's hard drive, a dedicated hardware server, or a home or office network. Cloud computing allows users with multiple computing devices, or a group of users working remotely on a collaborative project, to synchronize and access the same data

coauthor Also joint author. A writer who collaborates with one or more others in preparing a work

code (n) A symbol used to designate a particular data element. (v) To express in a form that the computer can use to retrieve the information

Collaborative Digital Reference Service CDRS. *See* QuestionPoint

collating 1. Putting all the parts of an item into correct order. 2. Checking an item to ensure it is correctly bound, with no part(s) missing

collation The physical description of a resource, including number of pages, illustrations, size, etc.

collected work Several separate works by different authors, or by the same author, selected by an editor for publication as a whole

collection assessment An evaluation of the quantity and quality of a collection

collection development Planning the acquisition of material to build a library collection for the short to long term, to meet the needs of library users

collection development policy A statement of the principles guiding a library's selection of new materials, receipt of gifts, exchanges, and weeding

collection maintenance All the tasks required to maintain the library collection for the use of readers—e.g., shelving, weeding, repair etc.

collection management The application of analytical methods to the development of a collection

collective biography Stories of the lives of a number of people

collective copyright licenses Standardized licensing agreements offered by copyright collection agencies to organizations (libraries, schools, government departments, etc.) that use copyrighted material. The licenses allow the agencies to collect royalty payments in bulk from the licensees and distribute them to their member copyright owners

collective title The title of a resource containing several works

collocation Arrangement that locates like material together

Colon Classification A classification scheme devised by S.R. Ranganathan, using numbers and letters, and a colon to separate different parts of the classification number

colophon A statement at the end of a resource giving information about title, author, publisher etc.

commentary Critical or explanatory comments on a work

commitment register A record of the projected cost of all library orders placed but not yet paid for

Committee on Cataloging: Description and Access CC:DA. The body within the American Library Association responsible for developing official ALA positions on additions to and revisions of descriptive cataloging standards http://www.ala.org/alcts/mgrps/camms/cmtes/ats-ccscat

Community Archive (NZ) *See* The Community Archive

community library A library set up and managed by a local community

compact disc CD. A disc on which sound is recorded by a laser and covered with a protective coating. The disc is then played by a laser beam. Often used when referring to recorded music—e.g., 'music CD'

compact disc read-only memory CD-ROM. A computer disc on which data is recorded and read using a laser. CD-ROM discs provide large capacity storage for computer programs and data, including audio, video and graphics. Cf USB flash drive

compact shelving Shelves on rollers and/or hinges that have to be moved in order to see the books; most often used in stacks

Compactus Trade name. A particular type of compact shelving

company library Also corporation library. A special library serving the needs of a business or an incorporated body

compendium A summary of a larger work, prepared by someone other than the author

compilation A work created by assembling material from other books

compiler 1. A person who selects and puts together material by other people. 2. A person who writes a reference work made up of many different entries, like a dictionary

complete stocktaking Checking the contents of the whole collection against the record of a library's holdings. Cf continuous stocktaking, sample stocktaking

composite author Each of the authors who contribute to a composite work in which each part is distinct

composite volume A volume containing separately published works

composite work An original work produced by two or more authors in which the contribution of each forms a separate and distinct part

compound surname A surname consisting of two or more proper names, sometimes connected by a hyphen or conjunction and/or preposition

comprehensive description In RDA, a bibliographic description for a resource as a whole (e.g., a map, a periodical, a collection of posters assembled by a library, or a kit consisting of a filmstrip, an audiotape and a teacher's manual). Cf analytical description, hierarchical description

computer literacy Familiarity with, and skills in using, the full range of computer functions

concept A term or subject heading that includes all ideas relating to it

concise Shortened, abbreviated

concordance An alphabetical index of the important words in a book, or the works of an author, with references to the phrases and passages in the text

condensed book A single volume in which an original work, usually fiction, is published in shortened form

Conference of Directors of National Libraries CDNL. An international forum of directors of all national libraries
www.cdnl.info/

Conference of Directors of National Libraries of Asia and Oceania CDNLAO. An organization that exchanges information and promotes cooperation for the development of libraries in Asia and Oceania
http://www.ndl.go.jp/en/cdnlao/index.html

conference proceedings The published papers given at a conference

confirming order An order for an item already received; authorizes payment

Congressional Research Service An administrative unit of the Library of Congress that provides research assistance to the federal legislature and other government agencies on issues related to proposed legislation
http://www.loc.gov/crsinfo/

connect time The time when a user is logged on to a computer system

Connexion OCLC's cataloging service, a suite of tools with built-in access to OCLC's WorldCat database with records from over 9000 libraries
http://www.oclc.org/connexion/

Conseil international des Archives / International Council on Archives ICA. The professional organization for the world archival community concerned with the preservation, development and use of the world's archival heritage
http://www.ica.org

CONSER Cooperative Online Serials Cataloging. An international cooperative online serials cataloging program, and a component of the Library of Congress's Program for Cooperative Cataloging
http://www.loc.gov/aba/pcc/conser/index.html

conservation Protecting library and other material from avoidable damage or deterioration without adding to or altering it. Cf preservation

consortium A partnership or association of institutions, databases or services with a shared objective. Cf library consortium

Consortium of European Research Libraries CERL. A group of European research libraries formed in 1992 to share resources and expertise with a view to improving access to and preservation of the European printed heritage
http://www.cerl.org/

container The outer casing of an item or group of items, that can be physically separated from those item(s) — e.g., the jewel case of a compact disc. Cf physical carrier

content 1. The essential matter or substance of a work. 2. The bibliographic information contained in a MARC record 3. In RDA, the physical characteristics (color, illustrations, scale, sound etc.) of the resource

content analysis Examination of the ideas and information in a work

content designation In MARC, all the tags, indicators and subfield codes that identify elements of the content of a record

content designator In MARC, a tag, indicator or subfield code that designates an element of the content of a record — e.g., **$a**London

contents 1. All the chapters, articles or separate works contained in a book or other resource. 2. All the loose items stored in a binder, case, or container

contents note A note in a bibliographic record, listing individual works within the resource described

contents page The page, usually at the front of a book or serial, that lists the contents in the order in which they appear

content type In RDA, the form of communication by which the content of a resource is expressed—e.g., spoken word, still image, text, etc.

contingency planning The development of a recovery plan to enable an organization to continue to function in the event of a disaster, including protection of computer systems, documents etc.

continuation 1. The remainder of a work completed by someone other than the original author. 2. A supplement to a previously published work

continuation order Also standing order, till forbid order. An order for all future issues of a serial title until the publisher is notified that no more issues are required

continuing professional development CPD. Ongoing education to develop knowledge, skills and personal qualities to enhance career-long professional performance

continuing resource A term used in AACR2 to describe a bibliographic resource issued over time and with no predetermined conclusion. RDA uses the terms 'serials' and 'integrated resources'

continuous pagination Numbering the pages of two or more volumes, parts or issues, as if they were a single volume

continuous revision Updating reference books by revising some of the text and illustrations with each printing. Cf revised edition

continuous stocktaking Checking the contents of one section of the library at a time against the record of the library's holdings. It may take several years to stocktake the whole collection. Cf complete stocktaking, sample stocktaking

contour map Also relief map. A map that shows elevations on the surface of the earth and beneath the oceans by means of contour lines, shading, etc.

contracting, contracting out Provision of library services by an individual or company not employed by the library. Cf outsourcing, independent librarian

contributor A person who writes a chapter of a book, an article of a periodical, or a part of an edited work

control field Also variable control field. A field in a MARC record with a tag 001-009 and no indicators or subfield codes. Control fields contain coded data used in processing the record

controlled access Limiting entry to a library or collection to specified clients

controlled vocabulary Terms found in an authoritative list of terms—e.g., Library of Congress Subject Headings, a database thesaurus

conventional name The popular but unofficial name of an institution—e.g., White House for the U.S. Presidency, Westminster Abby for the Collegiate Church of St Peter

CONZUL Council of New Zealand University Librarians. The organization of all New Zealand university librarians, providing a forum for discussion of issues relating to libraries and a mechanism for the coordination of activities that benefit the university community
http://www.universitiesnz.ac.nz/aboutus/sc/conzul/

cooperative cataloging, cooperative cataloguing Also shared cataloging. Sharing of catalog records by participating libraries

Cooperative Online Serials Cataloging CONSER. An international cooperative online serials cataloging program, and a component of the Library of Congress's Program for Cooperative Cataloging
http://www.loc.gov/aba/pcc/conser/

cooperative reference service An arrangement that extends a library's information service capability through interaction with and referral to other libraries or information centres

co-publishing Publishing different editions of the same work by more than one publisher in different countries or regions. Cf simultaneous publication

copy (v) 1. To make a duplicate. 2. To reproduce data from one location to another (n) 1. A single specimen of a manuscript or publication. 2. The result of a reproduction process

copy cataloging, copy cataloguing Copying cataloging details from an existing catalog record, and adding local location and holdings details

copy editing Checking a document for grammar, spelling and typographical errors, and inconsistency in style

copyright The right given by law to authors, composers or publishers to sell, reproduce or publish a work during a stated period of time. Cf Creative Commons

copyright agency Also copyright licensing agency, copyright collection society, copyright collective. An organization that administers the rights of copyright owners, who authorize the society to issue licenses for the use of their works and collect royalties on their behalf. Cf collective copyright licenses

Copyright Agency Limited CAL. The organization that represents Australian authors, artists and publishers in collecting photocopying and rights licensing fees
http://www.copyright.com.au/

Copyright Clearance Center CCC. A U.S. organization providing collective copyright licenses to corporate and academic users of copyrighted materials
http://www.copyright.com/

copyright collection society, copyright collective Also copyright licensing agency, copyright agency. An organization that administers the rights of copyright owners, who authorize the society to issue licenses for the use of their works and collect royalties on their behalf. Cf collective copyright licenses

copyright date The date associated with a claim of protection under copyright, identified in a resource by the symbol ©

copyright depository Also copyright library, deposit library. A library that is entitled by copyright law to receive publications on legal deposit

copyright legislation, copyright law The laws that protect the intellectual property rights of the creators of works. In the U.S, copyright law is contained in title 17 of the United States Code and the Digital Millennium Copyright Act, administered by the Copyright Office of the Library of Congress. In Canada, it is contained in the Copyright Act and Copyright Modernization Act. In Australia, copyright law is contained in the Copyright Act 1968 and the Copyright (Digital Agenda) Amendment Act 2000. In New Zealand, it is contained in the Copyright Act 1994. Court decisions that have interpreted the provisions of the relevant Act become part of copyright law

copyright library Also copyright depository, deposit library. A library that is entitled by copyright law to receive publications on legal deposit

copyright licensing agency Also copyright agency, copyright collection society, copyright collective. An organization that administers the rights of copyright owners, who authorize the society to issue licenses for the use of their works and collect royalties on their behalf. Cf collective copyright licenses

Copyright Licensing Agency CLA. The British company that provides collective copyright licenses on behalf of authors, publishers and artists https://www.cla.co.uk/

copyright piracy The reproduction of a work protected under copyright law, without permission from the copyright holder

copyright symbol The letter 'c' enclosed in a circle ©, printed on a resource along with a date and copyright owner's name to indicate that reproduction of the resource is protected under copyright law. In some countries this is required for copyright protection; in others the simple act of creating a resource protects its copyright

core collection 1. A collection that meets the basic needs of a library's primary users. 2. The collection assembled when a new library is established

core element In cataloging, an attribute that is part of RDA's set of minimum data required for describing a resource, or a person, family or corporate body associated with a resource

corporate body An organization or group of people identified by a particular name, and acting as an entity

corporation library Also company library. A special library serving the needs of a business or an incorporated body

correspondence Letters to and from a particular person, usually archived with that person's other papers

corrigenda Also errata. A printed list of corrections noticed after printing, usually on a slip of paper inserted or pasted between the pages

COSLA Chief Officers of State Library Agencies. An organization of the heads of U.S. state libraries, providing mechanisms for dealing with the issues faced by state librarians and directors responsible for statewide library development http://www.cosla.org/

Council of Australian University Librarians CAUL. The organization of librarians of all Australian universities, providing a forum for discussion of issues relating to libraries, and a mechanism for the coordination of activities that benefit the university community
http://www.caul.edu.au/

Council of New Zealand University Librarians CONZUL. The organization of all New Zealand university librarians, providing a forum for discussion of issues relating to libraries, and a mechanism for the coordination of activities that benefit the university community
http://www.universitiesnz.ac.nz/aboutus/sc/conzul/

Council on Library and Information Resources CLIR. An independent, non-profit organization based in the U.S. to enhance access to information in research, teaching and learning environments by working in collaboration with libraries, cultural institutions and communities of higher learning
http://www.clir.org/

country code 1. That section of an email or Internet address that identifies the country where the address is located — e.g., '*uk*' in the URL for the British Library, *www.bl.uk*. 2. A MARC code to indicate country of origin

country lending service Library service provided to users in rural areas who do not have access to a public library

coverage The range and depth of a library collection, catalog, or other database of library resources

cover title The title on the cover of a publication, that may differ from the authoritative version on the title page

CPD Continuing professional development. Ongoing education to develop knowledge, skills and personal qualities to enhance career-long professional performance

Creative Commons 1. An organization devoted to expanding the range of creative works available for others to build on legally and to share. 2. Copyright licenses created by Creative Commons that allow creators to specify the terms of use for their creations — e.g., which copyright rights they reserve, and which they waive
http://creativecommons.org

creator In RDA cataloging, a person, family or corporate body responsible for the creation of a work—e.g., writer of a book, compiler of a bibliography, composer of a musical work, artist, photographer etc.

credit A statement at the beginning or end of a film, videotape, or television program that identifies those responsible for creating it

credit note A note issued by a publisher or supplier showing the credit owing to a customer

critical abstract An abstract that evaluates the work cited

critical annotation An annotation that evaluates the source

CRKN Canadian Research Knowledge Network. A partnership of Canadian universities, dedicated to expanding access to scholarly research in digital formats. It builds on the Canadian National Site Licensing Project, under which over 2,200 journals and research databases were made available online http://crkn.ca/

CRL Center for Research Libraries. An international consortium of university, college and research libraries, that acquires and preserves print and digital primary resource materials from at-risk areas and makes them available to member institutions through interlibrary loan and electronic delivery http://www.crl.edu/

cross reference Direction from one term or entry to another

crosswalk Mapping from one format to another, e.g., from metadata to MARC

Cultural Ministers Council An intergovernmental forum for government ministers responsible for culture and the arts in Australia and New Zealand. Members collaborate on initiatives of national significance relating to art, film, culture, and collections of museums, galleries, libraries and archives http://cmc.arts.gov.au/

cumulate Gather together, as when monthly issues of a publication are gathered into an annual volume

cumulation 1. The progressive interfiling of resources arranged in a particular order. 2. The publication of a single integrated sequence of periodicals arranged in a particular order—e.g., an index

curiosa Books or pamphlets that address an unusual topic, especially erotica or pornography

current awareness bulletin CAB. A publication provided by a library to keep users up-to-date with information in their interest areas

current awareness service CAS. A service provided by a library to keep users up-to-date with information in their interest areas. Cf selective dissemination of information

current bibliography A bibliography that refers only to recently published sources. Cf retrospective bibliography

Current Index to Journals in Education CIJE. A U.S. index to education journals, published by ERIC, available through EBSCO
http://www.ebscohost.com/academic/eric

custody In archives, the care and official control of books, papers and documents

custom binding Special binding of a book, requested by a dealer, its owner, or the publisher

Cutter number A system of author numbers, devised by Charles A. Cutter, beginning with the first letter of the author's name and followed by numbers. Used in Library of Congress Classification for authors, titles and geographic areas. Cf book number

Cutter-Sanborn number An extension of the Cutter author number system, outlined in the Cutter-Sanborn Three-Figure Tables. Designed to maintain works with the same classification number in alphabetical order of author

cutting Also clipping. A page or pages cut out of a newspaper or some other printed material

cybrarian A contraction of cyberlibrarian, a librarian who works in information retrieval using the Internet and other online services

cybrary An online or highly technologically library

DACS Describing Archives: A Content Standard. Set of rules for describing archives, personal papers and manuscript collections of all material types, developed by the Society of American Archivists in 2004 and still current
http://files.archivists.org/pubs/DACS2E-2013.pdf

daily Issued every day, with the possible exception of Sundays

database A collection of records, usually in machine-readable format, each record being the required information about one resource

database management system DBMS. A software package for the creation and maintenance of databases

data compression Encoding data, or minimizing redundant information, so as to reduce the amount of storage needed in a computer. Cf zip

data conversion Translating data from one format to another, or from one medium (film, videotape) to another. Cf retrospective conversion. 2. Changing data from one file type to another—e.g., from a Word Perfect document (.wpd) to a Word document (.docx).

data element A single piece of information—e.g., date of publication

data element identifier In MARC, the lower-case letter that identifies a data element in a subfield—e.g., $a 25 pages : $b photographs

data field A field in a machine-readable record used to store data

data integrity The overall accuracy, completeness, and consistency of stored data, to ensure its validity and quality

data migration Moving data from one database or storage system to another

data mining Extracting useful information from online data. Cf data warehousing

data security The protection of data so that unauthorized users cannot access or copy it. Cf encryption

dataset A collection of data or databases

data warehousing Copying or collecting data from an organization's databases to a separate database, so that the data can be queried or analysed without disturbing the performance of the production system. Cf data mining

date due The date on or before which items should be returned to the library

date due slip A slip that is glued or inserted into the back of a book and is used to record when the book must be returned to the library

date of publication The earliest year in which the particular edition of the work was published; e.g., if a second edition was published in 1991, and reprinted without alteration in 1993, the date of publication of this edition is 1991

DBMS Database management system. A software package for the creation and maintenance of databases

DC Dublin Core Metadata Element Set. A standard for minimal description of document-like objects on the World Wide Web. Initiated by OCLC in 1995-96, it consists of 15 metadata elements: title, creator, subject, description, publisher, contributor, date, type, format, identifier, source, language, relation, coverage and rights
http://dublincore.org/

DCMI Dublin Core Metadata Initiative. An open forum engaged in the development of interoperable online metadata standards that support a broad range of purposes and business models
http://dublincore.org/

DDA demand driven acquisition. Also patron driven acquisition, PDA. An acquisition model usually applied to buying e-books, in which libraries include entries for possible acquisition in their catalog, and a title is triggered for purchase once a significant number of patrons request it

DDC Dewey Decimal Classification. A classification scheme devised by Melvil Dewey in 1873, using numbers to represent subjects
http://www.oclc.org/dewey/

deacidification Neutralising acid in the paper to prolong the life of a book or manuscript

dealer Someone who buys and sells new and used books and other materials

declassification Removing documents from official secrecy by altering their security status

dedicated computer A computer reserved for a specific function, often the provision of public access to a library's online catalog

dedication The author's inscription to a particular person or persons

deep Web Also invisible Web. Information on the Web that is not accessible via standard search engines

definitive edition An edition of the complete text of an author's work(s), edited and normally published after their death and regarded as authoritative

degaussing Also demagnetising. Removing excess magnetism from the heads of an audio or video recorder

delamination Removing adhesive plastic covering

delimiter 1. In MARC, a symbol used to introduce a new subfield. 2. A symbol indicating the end of a set of data—e.g., a record, field or subfield

demagnetising Also degaussing. Removing excess magnetism from an audio or video recorder

demand driven acquisition DDA. Also patron driven acquisition, PDA. An acquisition model usually applied to buying e-books, in which libraries include entries for possible acquisition in their catalog, and a title is triggered for purchase once a significant number of patrons request it

demand publishing A commercial service that supplies single copies of rare or out of print books, usually by making prints from a microfilmed master. Cf print on demand

dependent work A work related to a work already published by another author—e.g., a revised edition, commentary, or dramatization

deposit copy Also statutory copy. A free copy of a publication, sent to a copyright depository by the author or publisher to satisfy a legal requirement

deposit library, depository library Also copyright library, copyright depository. 1. A library that is entitled by copyright law to receive publications on legal deposit. 2. A library legally designated to receive government publications free of charge

deposit requirements The legal requirements of the copyright law as to how many copies and in which libraries published works are to be deposited

derivative work A work such as a translation or adaptation that alters the content of the original

derived authority record A name authority record generated from a bibliographic record, including a coded summary of the material associated with the person

Describing Archives: A Content Standard DACS. Set of rules for describing archives, personal papers and manuscript collections of all material types, developed by the Society of American Archivists in 2004 and still current http://files.archivists.org/pubs/DACS2E-2013.pdf

description Information about a work that can be derived from the work itself, including title, statement of responsibility, edition, publication details, physical description, series, and ISBN. Cf bibliographic description

descriptive cataloging, descriptive cataloguing The part of cataloging that describes a resource in terms of its physical (or electronic equivalent) details, and identifies and formulates access points

descriptive dictionary A dictionary that records words as they are used (and misused) without passing judgment. Cf prescriptive dictionary

descriptor A term used to identify a subject

deselection Also weeding. Discarding materials that are considered to be of no further use to the library, and removing their associated catalog records

desensitize, desensitise To reverse the magnetic field in security tape so that it will not activate the library's alarm system

desiderata Also waiting list, want list. A list of books and other materials wanted by a library, to be accepted when offered, or purchased when funds are available

desk schedule A roster of times when library staff work at the circulation desk, reference desk, or other point of interaction with clients

Dewey Decimal Classification DDC. A classification scheme, devised by Melvil Dewey in 1873, using numbers to represent subjects
http://www.oclc.org/dewey/

diacritic A mark, such as an accent, used with a letter to show how it is to be pronounced

diagram A plan or drawing that illustrates an idea, a process, or statistical information

dictionary An alphabetically arranged publication containing information about words, meanings, spelling, pronunciation, syllabication and usage

dictionary catalog, dictionary catalogue A catalog with all the entries arranged in a single alphabetical sequence. Cf divided catalog

digest An abridgment of a written work, usually prepared by a person other than the author of the original

digital library Also electronic library, e-library. A library in which many of the resources are in digital (machine-readable) format

Digital National Security Archive An online collection of U.S. foreign policy documents, available by subscription from ProQuest http://nsarchive.chadwyck.com

Digital Object Identifier DOI. An identification system for intellectual property in the digital environment, that provides a framework for managing intellectual content, linking customers with publishers, facilitating electronic commerce, and enabling automated copyright management. DOIs are persistent identifiers for electronic documents, articles and other resources http://www.doi.org

digital reference services Also ask a librarian services, virtual reference services. Reference assistance by library professionals, given online to library clients who may email, post questions, submit reference forms or engage in interactive chats or instant messaging

digital versatile disc, digital video disc DVD. A digitally-recorded CD-sized disc containing high-quality picture and sound performance of motion pictures

digitize, digitise To change analog data (e.g., printed text, images) into digital form which can be accessed using a computer

dimensions 1. Size. 2. In RDA, the measurement of the carrier and/or the container of a resource

diorama A miniature scene reproduced in three dimensions

directional enquiry An enquiry about where something is located

directory 1. An organizing structure for computer files. 2. A series of fixed-length entries following the leader in a MARC record, that define the content of the record. 3. A list of names of residents, organizations or companies in an area, providing various details—e.g., addresses. 4. A list of members of a particular profession or trade

disaster management plan, disaster plan Also emergency plan. A set of procedures to deal with a major emergency such as a flood or fire

discard (n) An item that has been withdrawn from a collection. (v) To withdraw an item from a collection and remove its record from the catalog

discharging Cancelling a loan record when an item is returned

discipline A very broad group of subjects in a classification scheme—e.g., social science

discography A list of sound recordings, often by the same performer(s)

discount Percentage of the recommended retail price of a book subtracted by the publisher or supplier when supplying the book to a retailer or information agency

discovery layer A library user interface using specialized software to simultaneously search the library's catalog, journal subscription services, institutional repositories, online resources etc. This provides a single point of access to the library's full collection, across bought, licensed and digital materials. Cf federated search

discussion group Also newsgroup. A group communicating on the Internet that can form on any topic or subject. Messages (news) can be sent electronically to the group for others to read and comment on

discussion list Also email list. An email-based means for discussion via the Internet, usually on specific topics

display case Also exhibit case. A rack for exhibiting any material that a library wants its users to notice

display constant In MARC, a word or words that precede some data when it is displayed, which are automatically generated by the MARC coding used—e.g., Summary:

dissertation Also thesis. A treatise prepared for the award of a diploma or degree, especially a postgraduate degree

Distributed National Collection The idea that the collections of all the nation's libraries jointly constitute the 'national collection', and that libraries cooperate in developing the collections

distribution Transporting, marketing and selling a resource

distribution statement In RDA, a statement identifying the place of distribution, distributor and date of distribution of a published resource

distributor An agent who has marketing rights for a resource

divided catalog, divided catalogue A catalog in which the entries are divided into separate sequences, usually author-title and subject. Cf dictionary catalog

DLL Downline loading, downloading. Copying data (e.g., bibliographic records) from one computer, such as an online database or the Internet, to a local system or terminal. Cf ULL

document (n) A work or portion of a work in any format, particularly print, electronic, or microform. (v) To acknowledge in writing the source of a quotation or idea that is not original

documentary A motion picture that records real events or conditions, often using historical film and photographs

documentation 1. The acquisition, organization, and distribution of specialized documents, usually technical or scientific. 2. A collection of documents about a specific subject. 3. Acknowledging the source of a quotation or idea that is not original. 4. Detailed written description of any procedure(s) or policies

documentation center, documentation centre An organization that receives, preserves, and indexes publications, usually in a particular discipline or field of research

document delivery The delivery of published and unpublished information by conventional and electronic means, including email and fax transmission. Cf interlibrary loan, interloan

document delivery service DDS. Supplying documents in hard copy, microform, or digitized format for a fee

DOI Digital Object Identifier. An identification system for intellectual property in the digital environment that aims to provide a framework for managing intellectual content, linking customers with publishers, facilitating electronic commerce, and enabling automated copyright management. DOIs are persistent identifiers for electronic documents, articles and other resources http://www.doi.org

domain name The address that identifies a site on the Internet—e.g., www.wcsu.edu, www.louvre.fr, www.abc.net.au

doubtful authorship Said of a work whose author is not certain, but which is attributed to an author or authors provisionally

downline loading DLL. Also downloading. Copying data (e.g., bibliographic records) from one computer, such as an online database or the Internet, to a local system or terminal. Cf upline loading

download To transfer a file from another computer to one's own computer

down time Time when a computer system is not operating

dpi Dots per inch. A measure of printer resolution that counts the dots that fit into a linear inch, The higher the dpi, the sharper and clearer the print

dramatization Adaptation of a written work for performance, live or on film

drop out White spots across the picture on a video tape, indicating that particles of iron oxide have dislodged with use

Dublin Core Metadata Element Set DC. A standard for minimal description of document-like objects on the World Wide Web. Initiated by OCLC in 1995-96, it consists of 15 metadata elements: title, creator, subject, description, publisher, contributor, date, type, format, identifier, source, language, relation, coverage and rights
http://dublincore.org/

Dublin Core Metadata Initiative DCMI. An open forum engaged in the development of interoperable online metadata standards that support a broad range of purposes and business models
http://dublincore.org/

dumb terminal A terminal that cannot process information, but just accesses and displays information from a computer server

duplicate (n) An additional copy of an item, that is not needed. (v) To copy

duplicates list Also exchange list. A list of unwanted or duplicate items circulated to other libraries to request before they are disposed of

durable paper Also acid-free paper, permanent paper. Paper that is pH neutral, and will last longer than paper with acid content

dust cover, dust jacket, dust wrapper Also book jacket, jacket, wrapper. Paper cover for a hard-bound book

DVD Digital versatile disc, digital video disc. A digitally recorded CD-sized disc containing high-quality picture and sound performance of motion pictures

EAC Encoded Archival Context. A metadata format designed to complement the Encoded Archival Description (EAD) by providing a separate description of the context under which archival records have been created

EACC East Asian Character Code. A standard code for representing Chinese, Japanese and Korean ideographs, used for cataloging these languages

EAD Encoded Archival Description. A metadata format for encoding archival finding aids (inventories, indexes or guides to archival and manuscript repositories). Used as an industry standard by the Library of Congress, National Library of Australia and other major collections
http://www.loc.gov/ead/

EALRGA East Asian Library Resources Group of Australia. An organization of librarians who aim to promote awareness of East Asian library resources and librarianship in Australia, and enhance interaction among library professionals, scholars and anyone interested in East Asian studies
http://www.ealrga.org.au/

East Asian Character Code EACC. A standard code for representing Chinese, Japanese and Korean ideographs, used for cataloging these languages

East Asian Library Resources Group of Australia EALRGA. An organization of librarians who aim to promote awareness of East Asian library resources and librarianship in Australia, and enhance interaction among library professionals, scholars and anyone interested in East Asian studies
http://www.ealrga.org.au/

e-book electronic book. A book published in electronic format and made available via the Internet or for use on a portable electronic device

e-book reader electronic book reader, e-reader. A device for reading electronic books

e-book software Computer programs developed to allow e-books to be read on a computer screen. They provide features such as bookmarking, changing the font size, etc.

ebrary A commercial e-book vendor service of ProQuest, offering electronic resources by purchase, subscription, loan or via demand driven acquisition
http://www.ebrary.com/

edition All the copies of a work produced from the same original

edition statement The part of a bibliographic description that indicates the particular edition of the resource—e.g., revised, illustrated, student, abridged

editor Person who prepares another person's work for publication

editorial page Page—e.g., of a serial, that contains the opinion of an editor

educational lending right A payment made to authors by the Australian government in respect of their works lent by educational libraries
http://arts.gov.au/literature/lending_rights

Educational Resources Information Center ERIC. U.S. database of educational information, including journal articles and full documents. Cf Current Index to Journals in Education
http://eric.ed.gov/

EH&S Environmental health and safety. Also OH&S, occupational health and safety, WHS, workplace health and safety. Legal requirements for ensuring a safe workplace

e-journal electronic journal. A periodical published in electronic format, and made available via the Internet

electronic book e-book. A book published in electronic format and made available via the Internet or for use on a portable electronic device

electronic book reader Also e-book reader, e-reader. A device for reading electronic books

electronic journal e-journal. A periodical published in electronic format, and made available via the Internet

electronic library Also digital library, e-library. A library in which many of the resources are in digital (machine-readable) format

electronic list e-list. An automated electronic mail serving system

electronic mail email. Sending and receiving messages electronically

electronic publishing Making information available in electronic form, usually on the Internet

electronic publishing on demand Also EPOD, print on demand, POD, publishing on demand. A type of publishing using digital printing technology, in which a book or other publication is printed on an as-needed basis, allowing small print runs and dispensing with the need for warehousing stock

electronic record Records held in digital form on magnetic (e.g., discs, tapes) or optical (e.g., CD-ROMs) storage media

electronic reserve e-reserve A collection of online materials in an academic library, to which access is restricted to users with a password

electronic resource e-resource. Any source of information available electronically, usually on the Internet

electronic resource management system A library management system focusing on managing and providing access to e-books, e-journals and other electronic resources

electronic style A bibliographic format for citing information available electronically. Cf APA style, Chicago style, MLA style, Harvard style

element In cataloging, a distinct piece of bibliographic information. Cf core element

elephant folio An extremely large-format book

e-library Also digital library, electronic library. A library in which many of the resources are in digital (machine-readable) format

e-list electronic list. An automated electronic mail serving system

email electronic mail. Sending and receiving messages electronically

email list Also discussion list. An email-based means for discussion via the Internet, usually on specific topics

emergency plan Also disaster management plan, disaster plan. A set of procedures to deal with a major emergency such as a flood or fire

encapsulation Sealing a flat document between two sheets of transparent plastic film to protect it from damage

Encoded Archival Context EAC. A metadata format designed to complement the Encoded Archival Description (EAD) by providing a separate description of the context under which archival records have been created

Encoded Archival Description EAD. A metadata format for encoding archival finding aids (inventories, indexes or guides to archival and manuscript repositories). Used as an industry standard by the Library of Congress, National Library of Australia and other major collections
http://www.loc.gov/ead/

encryption The process of transforming data into random streams of bits to prevent unauthorized access

encumbrance A sum charged to cover a prior commitment to purchase material or equipment

encyclopedia, encyclopaedia 1. A systematic summary of all significant knowledge. 2. A summary of the knowledge of one subject. Usually arranged alphabetically. Cf Wikipedia

end matter The material at the end of a work, following the text—e.g., appendices, index

endnote A note at the end of a chapter or a work, with additional information, usually a citation. Cf footnote

EndNote Reference management software produced by Thomson Reuters, used to manage bibliographies and references when writing essays and articles. Cf ProCite
http://endnote.com/

endowment A fund made up of donations and bequests, invested to provide annual interest over many years. Many American scholarships and grants are funded via endowments

end papers The papers that join the front and back cover of a book to the central section

end processing Also process, processing, physical processing. To prepare an item for use in the library or for loan. This can include affixing library stamps, barcodes, call number labels, dust covers, etc.

end-user 1. A person other than a library staff member, who uses the resources of the library. 2. The person for whom an information search is made

enhanced authority record A name authority record including information from all the bibliographic records associated with the person

enquiry desk Also help desk, information desk, readers' adviser's desk, reference desk. The area of a library where staff help people to use the library and answer requests for information

entity The FRBR (*Functional Requirements for Bibliographic Records*) term for materials, people or concepts that are the basis for bibliographic or authority descriptions. FRBR identifies three Groups of entities (Group 1: works, expressions, manifestations, items; Group 2: persons, families, corporate bodies; Group 3: concepts, objects, events, places)

entry A record of a resource in a catalog or other bibliographic list or database

entry element That part of a name or topic under which it will be found in a catalog or bibliography

enumerative classification A type of classification that attempts to spell out (enumerate) all the single and composite subjects required—e.g., Library of Congress Classification

environmental health and safety EH&S. Also OH&S, occupational health and safety, WHS, workplace health and safety. Legal requirements for ensuring a safe workplace

environmental scan A broad survey of current topics in a particular discipline

ephemera 1. Material of current interest that is expected to be stored for a limited time—e.g., pamphlets, clippings. 2. Material intended to be short-lived, but which is retained to reflect a period in time

epigraph A brief quotation that appears at the front of a book, or at the beginning of a chapter, to convey the author's intention

epilogue The final section of a literary work, reflecting on its meaning, or imagining the future of the characters in it

EPOD Electronic publishing on demand. Also print on demand, POD, publishing on demand. A type of publishing using digital printing technology, in which a book or other publication is printed on an as-needed basis, allowing small print runs and dispensing with the need for warehousing stock

e-reader Also e-book reader, electronic book reader. A device for reading electronic books

e-reserve electronic reserve. A collection of online materials in an academic library, to which access is restricted to users with a password

e-resource electronic resource. Any source of information available electronically, usually on the Internet

ERIC Educational Resources Information Center. U.S. database of educational information, including journal articles and full documents. Cf Current Index to Journals in Education
http://eric.ed.gov/

erotica Literary works intended to arouse sexual desire in a reader, and that have artistic value and integrity. Cf pornography

errata Singular erratum. Also corrigenda. A printed list of corrections noticed after printing, usually on a slip of paper inserted or pasted between the pages

essay A short prose composition, usually dealing with a single theme or subject for academic assessment, or as a personal point of view

et al. An abbreviation of the Latin *et alii* (and others). In AACR2 cataloging, used to replace names in a statement of responsibility when there are more than three authors

etymology The derivation of a word, its origin and history

excerpt A lengthy verbatim selection taken from a literary or other work, usually longer than a quotation

exchange A way of acquiring material in return for a different set of material. Usually undertaken when libraries have difficulty acquiring material from particular countries, or when hard currency is scarce

exchange list Also duplicates list. A list of unwanted or duplicate items circulated to other libraries to request before they are disposed of

exciter lamp The lamp in a motion projector that provides light to convert the encoded sound track to electrical signals which are fed to the amplifier

exhibit case Also display case. A rack for exhibiting any material that a library wants its users to notice

exhibition catalog, exhibition catalogue A type of art book containing a commentary and reproductions of visual art works being exhibited in a museum or gallery

ex libris A Latin phrase meaning 'From the books of...' followed by the owner's name on a bookplate

explanatory reference A longer 'see' or 'see also' reference that explains when a heading or headings should be used

export To send data from one computer application to another—e.g., exporting bibliographic records from an online union catalog to an individual member library's computer system

expression In RDA, one of the Group 1 entities described in *Functional Requirements for Bibliographic Records* as a particular intellectual or artistic realization of a work, or, the means by which a work is expressed—e.g., spoken word, language translation, with illustrations, etc. Cf item, manifestation, work

expurgated Amended by removing offensive or objectionable matter

extension A suffix added to a filename to indicate the type of file—e.g., .txt for a plain text file or .html for a file in HTML script

extent Also extent of resource. In RDA, the number and type of units and/or subunits making up a resource

extent of item In AACR2, the number and specific material designation of the parts of the item being described

extent of resource Also extent. In RDA, the number and type of units and/or subunits making up a resource

extract A lengthy passage in the main text of a book, usually indented to signal the fact that it is quoted from a different book or other source

extranet A website serving suppliers, vendors, customers or other businesses rather than the general public, usually accessible only with a password

e-zine Also zine, web-zine. An online magazine or newsletter, distributed by email or posted on a website

facet 1. Classification: An aspect or orientation of a topic. 2. Records management: A group of terms that share a common characteristic

Faceted Application of Subject Terminology FAST. An adaptation by OCLC of Library of Congress Subject Headings to produce a faceted schema that is easier to understand, control, apply, and use
http://www.oclc.org/research/activities/fast.html

faceted classification A type of classification that allows for notation to be built up by the use of tables and other parts of the schedules. All modern classification schemes are faceted to a degree. Colon Classification is the definitive faceted classification scheme

facsimile 1. An exact copy. 2. Also fax. Transmission of a document via a telephone line

Factiva A business database owned by Dow Jones, providing full-text news, business and company information
http://new.dowjones.com/factiva/

fair dealing Making a copy, for the purpose of research or study, of one or more articles on the same subject matter in a periodical publication or, in the case of any other work, of a reasonable portion of a work—i.e., 10% of the total number of pages, or one chapter

fair use Copying of copyrighted material for a limited purpose such as to comment on, criticize, or parody a copyrighted work. The copyright acts of various countries contain different fair use provisions

false drop, false combination An irrelevant entry or record retrieved in an online database search—e.g., a search for the Native American people 'Mohawks' will also retrieve information about unusual hairstyles

false imprint Also fictitious imprint. An imprint that is invented to evade legal and/or other restrictions, or to conceal the author's identity

fascicle, fascicule Each part of a book or other printed resource that is issued in instalments

FAST Faceted Application of Subject Terminology. An adaptation by OCLC of Library of Congress Subject Headings to produce a faceted schema that is easier to understand, control, apply, and use
http://www.oclc.org/research/activities/fast.html

fax Also facsimile. Transmission of a document via a telephone line

fax card A card installed in a personal computer that enables the user to send and receive faxes directly from and to the computer

FDsys The U.S. Government Printing Office's Federal Digital System, that provides free online access to official publications from the U.S. federal government. Cf SuDocs number
http://www.gpo.gov/fdsysinfo/aboutfdsys

federated search A technology that lets users search multiple databases simultaneously using one search query, then view the results in a single integrated list. Cf meta search engine, discovery layer

Fédération Internationale des Archives de Télévision / International Federation of Television Archives FIAT/IFTA. Set up in 1977 to encourage cooperation among television archives, libraries, and all those engaged in the preservation and exploitation of moving image materials; and to establish international standards for audiovisual media archive management
http://fiatifta.org/

feedback Response to an activity or product

festschrift A publication in honor of a person

FIAF International Federation of Film Archives. An association of the world's leading film archives founded in 1938 with the aim of ensuring the proper preservation and screening of motion pictures
http://www.fiafnet.org/

FIAT/IFTA Fédération Internationale des Archives de Télévision / International Federation of Television Archives. Set up in 1977 to encourage cooperation among television archives, libraries, and all those engaged in the preservation and exploitation of moving image materials; and to establish international standards for audiovisual media archive management
http://fiatifta.org/

fiche Also microfiche. A microfilmed transparency about the size and shape of a filing card, that may have on it many pages of print

fiction Prose writing that is the product of the author's imagination

fictitious imprint Also false imprint. An imprint that is invented to evade legal and/or other restrictions, or to conceal the author's identity

field 1. Unit of information in a MARC record that corresponds to an area of description or other piece of information—e.g., access point. 2. Element of a record in a database

Fiji Library Association FLA. The professional association of Fijian librarians http://www.fla.org.fj/

file 1. Systematically arranged records. 2. The container in which records are arranged. 3. A document created on a computer

file-as-is File as the entry looks and not as it sounds—e.g., 'Mr' is not filed as 'Mister'

filename The title given by the user of a data file to identify and retrieve it

file type The kind of file—e.g., program file, text file, image file

filing code A set of rules for arranging records in a file

filing indicator In MARC, the indicator that tells the computer how many characters to ignore when filing

film Motion picture of 8mm, 16mm or 35mm width that can be projected, and may contain a sound track

film library A special library that collects mainly motion picture films and materials related to film-making

filmloop A length of motion picture film joined in a loop, so that it can be projected continuously

filmstrip A strip of 16mm or 35mm film containing a sequence of pictures, with or without text, that can be projected

finding list A summary list of the resources in a library or archive collection in which each resource is represented only by a brief entry, usually author, title, and location

fine A monetary penalty imposed on a user who returns library material after the due date

finite integrating resource A bibliographic resource that is changed by being updated; not intended to continue indefinitely—e.g., a newsletter of a conference. Cf ongoing integrating resource

Firefox An open source web browser developed by Mozilla
http://www.mozilla.org/

firewall A security system on a server to the Internet, that prevents unauthorized access from the Net to an organization's own network

firm order An order placed with a dealer that specifies a price and a delivery time, which may not be exceeded unless the library agrees

first-line index An index of the first lines of poems or songs, in alphabetical order—e.g., *Hoffman's index to poetry*

FirstSearch Also OCLC FirstSearch. A collection of reference databases available via the Internet from OCLC
http://www.oclc.org/firstsearch/

first summary of Dewey Decimal Classification The 10 classes, each of which represents a broad discipline or group of disciplines

fiscal Relating to financial matters

fixed field data Data in a MARC record where the size of the field is predetermined

fixed length field A field that has its length determined in advance. Cf variable length field

fixed location A way of arranging library materials in which resources are shelved in a prescribed place and new resources are added at the end of the sequence

fixed shelving A shelving system in which each shelf is permanently attached to the framework of a bookcase. Cf adjustable shelving

FLA Fiji Library Association. The professional association of Fijian librarians
http://www.fla.org.fj/

flap One of the two ends of the jacket that wraps around the cover of a hardcover book

flash card A stiff card bearing a letter, word, phrase, or symbol, used in teaching

flash drive Also USB flash drive, memory stick, thumb drive. A small removable and rewritable data storage device that plugs into a USB port, used for storage, backup and transfer of computer files. Often used in preference to CD-ROMs because of its high storage capacity, small size, durability and reliability. Cf CD-ROM

floating collection A collection circulated from a central library to a number of small associated libraries or branches

Florence Agreement UNESCO agreement adopted in 1952 that reduces trade barriers to the international export and import of books, documents and other educational, scientific and cultural material

fly leaf The blank sheet at the beginning or end of a book

fly-title Also bastard title, half title. The brief title of a book that appears on the leaf preceding the title page

FOI Freedom of information. The citizen's right to access information held by their government

FOIA Freedom of Information Act (U.S.). Law passed by the U.S. Congress, under which citizens may apply in writing for particular official information. Copies of the documents must be supplied within a specified period http://www.foia.gov

FOI Act Freedom of Information Act 1982 (Australia). Australian law, reformed in 2010, under which individuals can request access to documents containing their personal information or other information from Australian Government ministers and most government agencies http://www.oaic.gov.au/freedom-of-information/freedom-of-information

folio 1. The size of a book, usually over 30 cm. Some libraries refer to these as 'large' books. 2. A book that is printed on sheets of paper folded once. 3. The individual leaf of a book

font A typeface of a particular design, size, and style (e.g., Arial, 12 pt, bold)

footnote A note at the bottom of a page with additional information, usually a citation. Cf endnote

foreword A brief statement of the reasons for the book, usually by the author or editor. It appears after the title page and before the introduction

form 1. The way in which bibliographic text is arranged—e.g., dictionary. 2. Type of literary work—e.g., poetry, drama

format (n) 1. Appearance of a publication—its size, paper, type, binding etc. 2. Layout or presentation of items in machine-readable form. 3. Physical type of an audiovisual resource—e.g., slide, filmstrip etc. 4. Physical organization of a catalog—e.g., card, microfiche, online etc. (v) 1. To arrange text and/or images on a screen to prepare it for printing. 2. To prepare a computer disc so that it can receive data

format of notated music In RDA, the musical or physical layout of the content of a resource that is presented in the form of musical notation—e.g., score, piano conductor part. AACR2 uses the term 'musical presentation statement'

form class Used for literature. Resources are classified not according to subject, but according to their literary form—e.g., poetry, drama

form division Used for works on any subject that are presented in a particular bibliographic form—e.g., dictionary, periodical

forthcoming To be published soon

foxing Yellowish-brown spots on the pages of old books

FRAD Functional Requirements for Authority Data. A framework for relating the data recorded in library authority records to the needs of users, enabling them to find, identify, contextualize and justify the information collected. With FRBR, an integral concept underlying RDA cataloging guidelines. Cf RDA, FRBR, FRSAD
http://www.ifla.org/publications/functional-requirements-for-authority-data

FRBR Functional Requirements for Bibliographic Records. A framework that identifies and clearly defines the entities of interest to users of bibliographic records, the attributes of each entity, and the types of relationships that operate between entities. The conceptual model underlying RDA cataloging guidelines. Cf RDA, FRAD, FRSAD
http://www.ifla.org/publications/functional-requirements-for-bibliographic-records

freedom of information FOI. The citizen's right to access information held by their government

Freedom of Information Act FOIA (U.S.). Law passed by the U.S. Congress in 1966, under which citizens may apply in writing for particular official information. Copies of the documents must be supplied within a specified period
http://www.foia.gov

Freedom of Information Act 1982 (FOI Act) (Australia). Australian law, reformed in 2010, under which individuals can request access to documents containing their personal information or other information from Australian Government ministers and most government agencies
http://www.oaic.gov.au/freedom-of-information/freedom-of-information

freedom of information legislation The laws that enshrine citizens' right to access information held by their governments. Many countries have enacted such legislation. In the U.S., freedom of information law is contained in the Freedom of Information Act. In Canada, it is contained in the Access to Information Act. In Australia, freedom of information is covered in the Freedom of Information Act 1982 and its amendments. In New Zealand, it is contained in the Official Information Act 1982. Provisions on what is covered by these laws, and how to access information through them, differ from country to country

Freedom to Read Foundation An organization that works closely with the American Library Association to promote and protect freedom of speech, freedom of the press, the public's right of access to libraries, and the right of libraries to collect and make available all legal creative works
http://www.ftrf.org/

free-floating subdivision A subheading in Library of Congress Subject Headings that is applied to one or more categories of main headings—e.g., Periodicals

free-standing shelving A shelving system that stands on its own, independent of any external support. Cf wall shelving

free text searching Searching for text appearing anywhere in the record

freeware Software that is made available without cost, usually via the Internet by the owner of the copyright. Cf shareware

frequency Interval between issues of a serial—e.g., weekly, quarterly

Fresnel lens A lens used in an overhead projector to concentrate the light

Friends of the Library Volunteer organizations that support a particular library through fundraising and promotional activities

frontispiece An illustration facing or preceding the title page

front matter Also preliminary pages. All parts of a book before the first page of the text

FRSAD Functional Requirements for Subject Authority Data. A conceptual framework for relating subject information to bibliographic records, enabling users to find, identify select and explore relationships between and among subjects. Like FRBR and FRAD, an integral concept underlying RDA cataloging guidelines. Cf RDA, FRAD, FRBR
http://www.ifla.org/files/assets/classification-and-indexing/functional-requirements-for-subject-authority-data/frsad-final-report.pdf

full-text Complete document

full-text database A database that contains complete texts of resources

full-text searching Also full-text retrieval. Online searching in which every word of a document can be retrieved

Functional Requirements for Authority Data FRAD. A framework for relating the data recorded in library authority records to the needs of users, enabling them to find, identify, contextualize and justify the information collected. Along with FRBR and FRSAD, an integral concept underlying RDA cataloging guidelines. Cf RDA, FRBR, FRSAD
http://www.ifla.org/publications/functional-requirements-for-authority-data

Functional Requirements for Bibliographic Records FRBR. A framework that identifies and clearly defines the entities of interest to users of bibliographic records, the attributes of each entity, and the types of relationships that operate between entities. The conceptual basis underlying RDA cataloging guidelines. Cf RDA, FRAD, FRSAD
http://www.ifla.org/publications/functional-requirements-for-bibliographic-records

Functional Requirements for Subject Authority Data FRSAD. A conceptual framework for relating subject information to bibliographic records, enabling users to find, identify, select and explore relationships between and among subjects. Like FRBR and FRAD, an integral concept underlying RDA cataloging guidelines. Cf RDA, FRAD, FRBR
http://www.ifla.org/files/assets/classification-and-indexing/functional-requirements-for-subject-authority-data/frsad-final-report.pdf

fuzzy logic An enhancement of searching to enable a user to find like or related words

gate The part of a film projector where the film passes between the light beam and the magnifying lens

gatefold An illustration that is larger than the volume in which it is bound and must be unfolded to be seen

gateway 1. A computer or program that connects two or more networks and enables users to access one network from another. 2. Also portal, subject gateway. An entry point to the Internet that provides access to electronic information including websites, ftp sites, databases and indexes to print resources in a subject area—e.g., agriculture

gazette A periodically published newssheet recording current events. 2. A journal issued officially by a government

gazetteer A geographical directory listing places, their locations and information about them

GEDI Generic Electronic Document Interchange. The international standard (ISO 17933) specifying a format for exchange of electronic document copies between computer systems. Used in systems that support interlibrary loan and document transmission applications
www.iso.org/cate/d31634.html

genealogy The study of the ancestry of an individual, family, or group

generalia class In DDC, used for very general topics and comprehensive combinations of topics—e.g., current affairs, general encyclopedias

General International Standard Archival Description ISAD(G). Set of rules for archival description developed by the International Council on Archives in 2000. Cf Encoded Archival Description (EAD), Rules for Archival Description (RAD), Describing Archives: a Content Standard (DACS)
http://www.ica.org/10207/standards/isadg-general-international-standard-archival-description-second-edition.html

general material designation GMD. A concept in AACR2 used to describe the broad category of material to which a resource belongs—e.g., sound recording. RDA divides this concept into three elements: content type, media type and carrier type. Cf specific material designation

Generic Electronic Document Interchange GEDI. The international standard (ISO 17933) specifying a format for exchange of electronic document copies between computer systems. Used in systems that support interlibrary loan and document transmission applications
www.iso.org/cate/d31634.html

genre A category of literature—e.g., novel, fantasy, science fiction, poetry

Geographical Information System GIS. A system of hardware and software used for storage, retrieval, mapping, and analysis of geographic data

geographic name Name of a place—country, state, city, town, suburb etc.

geographic subdivision Also local subdivision. The subdivision of a class or subject heading by place (region, country, state, city, etc.)

geospatial data Information containing a location or map—e.g., including latitude and longitude

ghost Also bibliographic ghost. A work or edition of a work recorded in bibliographies, catalogs and other sources, which may not exist

ghost writer A person who writes a work in the name of another person who is usually famous but not a professional writer

GIF Graphics interchange format. A graphics format widely used to encode and exchange graphics files on the Internet

gift An item received by a library as a donation

GILS Global Information Locator Service. Metadata format created by the U.S. federal government to provide a means of locating information generated by government agencies on the Web
http://www.gils.net/

GIS Geographical Information System. A system of hardware and software used for storage, retrieval, mapping, and analysis of geographic data

Global Books in Print Also Books in Print. Listing of over 20 million in-print, out-of-print, and forthcoming book, audio, and video titles, available online, on CD-ROM and in print. Available in U.S. edition or Global Edition
http://www.booksinprint.com/   or   http://www.bowker.com

Global Information Locator Service GILS. Metadata format created by the U.S. federal government to provide a means of locating information generated by government agencies on the Web
http://www.gils.net/

Global Reference Network GRN. A collective of libraries and librarians formed to assist the development of a new collaborative online reference service, QuestionPoint, developed by the Library of Congress and OCLC
http://www.loc.gov/rr/digiref/

glossary An alphabetical list of definitions

GMD general material designation. A concept in AACR2 used to describe the broad category of material to which a resource belongs—e.g., sound recording. RDA divides this concept into three elements: content type, media type and carrier type. Cf specific material designation

GOLD Government On-Line Directory. The official guide to the Australian Government's structure and personnel, available on the Web
http://gold.gov.au/

Google A service that locates information on the World Wide Web
http://www.google.com

Google Chrome Web browser software by Google
www.google.com/chrome

Google Scholar A free web search engine that facilitates searching of scholarly literature whether in digital or physical form, online, in libraries or available from commercial publishers. There is an emphasis on full-text journal articles and reports, which can be downloaded or purchased
http://scholar.google.com.au/intl/en/scholar/about.html

government discussion paper *See* green paper

government document A publication that carries the authority of a national, federal or state government, such as bills, statutes, treaties, statistics, and resolutions

Government On-Line Directory GOLD. The official guide to the Australian Government's structure and personnel, available on the Web
http://gold.gov.au/

government policy paper *See* white paper

government publication A document prepared for or by a government agency, which is published and distributed for public information

Governor General's Literary Awards Canada's national literary awards, administered by the Canada Council, honoring the best of Canadian literature in either English or French
http://ggbooks.canadacouncil.ca/en/about-apropos.aspx

GovPubs Australian Government Publications Guide. A guide to selected types of Australian government publications, such as acts, Hansards, gazettes and parliamentary papers, that are located in Australia's national, state and territory libraries or available on the Internet. The database is searchable but no longer maintained
http://www.nla.gov.au/govpubs/index.html

grace period In America, the period after the due date when a borrower may return overdue items without having to pay a fine

graduate library A university library that contains the major research collections required by graduate students and faculty

gramophone record Also phonograph record, vinyl record. A sound disc made of vinyl plastic, with sound grooves pressed into the surface

grant Funding from a government, a foundation, or other organization, usually to support a specific project

grant-in-aid In America, income from state or federal government funds in support of designated library programs or normal operations

graphic novel A book presented in comic-strip format, intended for either adults or children. Cf manga

graphics The pictorial representation of information using illustrations, diagrams, photographs, and maps

graphics interchange format GIF. A graphics format widely used to encode and exchange graphics files on the Internet

gratis Provided free

green paper A report put out by the government, designed to stimulate discussion and canvass agreement before drafting an official policy document Cf white paper

grey literature Informally published materials, such as reports or working papers, that may be difficult to trace through conventional acquisitions sources because they are not published commercially or not widely accessible

GRN Global Reference Network. A collective of libraries and librarians formed to assist the development of a new collaborative online reference service, QuestionPoint, developed by the Library of Congress and OCLC http://www.loc.gov/rr/digiref/

Group 1 entities In FRBR and RDA, the products of intellectual or artistic endeavor that are named or described in bibliographic records. These Group 1 entities are: work, expression, manifestation and item (WEMI)

Group 2 entities In FRBR and RDA, entities responsible for the intellectual and artistic content, the physical production and dissemination, or the ownership or custodianship of Group 1 entities. These Group 2 entities are: persons, families and corporate bodies

Group 3 entities In FRBR and RDA, entities that serve as the subjects of intellectual and artistic endeavors. These Group 3 entitles are: concepts, objects, events, places, and Group 1 and Group 2 entities as subjects

guidebook A reference book that provides useful information for travellers to a city, country, region, or other location, or for visitors to a museum, gallery or similar site

hagiography 1. A written account of the life of a saint. 2. The branch of literature concerned with the lives of saints. 3. Inappropriately deferential writing

half title Also bastard title, fly-title. The brief title of a book that appears on the leaf preceding the title page

half yearly Also semiannual. Issued every six months

handbill A sheet of paper on which an advertisement or announcement is printed, distributed by hand

handbook A concise ready reference source of information for a particular field of knowledge

Hansard The official report of proceedings in parliaments

Hans Christian Andersen Awards Awards made every two years by the International Board on Books for Young People (IBBY) to a living author and a living illustrator who have made a distinguished contribution to international literature for young people
http://www.ibby.org/

hardback, hard bound, hard cover Also cased. Bound in cloth- or paper-covered boards. Cf paperback

hardware 1. Audiovisual equipment—e.g., slide projector, 16mm projector etc. 2. Computer equipment—e.g., computer, monitor, keyboard etc. Cf software

Harvard style A format for citing references using author and date, developed by Harvard University. Cf APA style, Chicago style, MLA style

HathiTrust digital library A repository of both public domain and in-copyright digitized books and journals from research institutions and library collections. The Trust aims to build a comprehensive archive of published literature from around the world and devise strategies for managing and developing it
http://www.hathitrust.org/

head An electromagnet in an audio or video recorder that magnetizes, demagnetizes or 'reads' the magnetic pattern on audio or video tape

head band A piece of cloth stitched at the top of the book spine to reinforce it and for decoration

heading Used in AACR2, a name, word or phrase at the top of a catalog entry to provide an access point. RDA uses the term 'authorized access point'

help desk Also enquiry desk, information desk, readers' adviser's desk, reference desk. The area of a library where staff help people to use the library and answer requests for information

Her Majesty's Stationery Office *See* The Stationery Office

hierarchical classification Classification in which the division of subjects is from the most general to the most specific—e.g., Dewey Decimal Classification

hierarchical description In RDA, a bibliographic description that combines a comprehensive description of the whole resource with analytical descriptions of one or more of its parts. Cf comprehensive description, analytical description

hierarchy 1. The ranked order of subjects in a classification scheme. 2. The order of subordinate bodies in a multi-level corporate body

hit 1. The location of a relevant item in a computer database. 2. A match in a search for a bibliographic record

hold Item taken from the shelves and held for a period for a client

holdings Stock of a library or information centre

holdings note Information about the stock of a library or information centre, usually on a catalog

holdings policy Also keeping policy. A library's policy on the length of time, location, disposal etc. of library material, especially serials

holdings rate The percentage of items requested by users of a library that are held in its collections

hollow back Covering of a hardback book that allows the spine to move freely away from the book when it is opened

homebound service Also housebound service. Library service providing books and other library materials to clients who are unable to come to the library

Horizon An integrated client/server library management system, developed and distributed by SirsiDynix
http://www.sirsidynix.com/horizon

host organization, host organisation The organization of which a special library is part—e.g., the corporation that maintains a library for its employees

housebound service Also homebound service. Library service providing books and other library materials to clients who are unable to come to the library

house organ A periodical issued by an organization for the information of its employees or clients

house style A publisher's particular standards of presentation, grammar, abbreviation, and citation

HP Records Manager Formerly TRIM. An automated record-keeping system for paper and electronic records, widely used in Australian organizations
http://www.autonomy.com/html/participate/rm8/html/index.html

HTML Hypertext mark-up language. The standard language used to create documents on the World Wide Web

hyperlink Also link. A keyword, phrase or graphic on the Web that connects to another web page

hypertext Information connected via links in the text, with a computer automating movement from one piece of information to another

Hypertext Mark-up Language HTML. A set of commands or tags used to create documents on the World Wide Web; now the standard language of the Web

IASL International Association of School Librarianship. Founded to promote school library provision all over the world, and maintained by individual and organizational members
http://www.iasl-online.org/

IATUL International Association of Scientific and Technological University Libraries. An international forum for the exchange of ideas relevant to librarianship in technological universities throughout the world, with membership open to library directors and senior managers
http://www.iatul.org/

IBBY International Board on Books for Young People. An organization to promote global understanding through children's books, comprising national sections working within their own countries to promote children's books
http://www.ibby.org

ibid. Abbreviation for Latin *ibidem* (in the same place). Used in a footnote to avoid repeating the title of the work immediately above

ICA International Council on Archives / Conseil international des Archives. The professional organization for the world archival community, dedicated to the preservation, development and use of the world's archival heritage
http://www.ica.org/

ICML International Congress on Medical Librarianship. A conference held every 4-5 years under the auspices of IFLA, to facilitate the flow of information and ideas in health sciences librarianship

ICOLC International Coalition of Library Consortia. An informal group of higher education consortia that serves as an information resource about new technologies, electronic services, pricing, and related issues
http://icolc.net/

icon A small graphic on a computer that represents a program, file etc.

identifier In RDA, a string of characters used to uniquely identify a resource—e.g., an ISBN, a URL—or to identify a person, family or corporate body associated with a resource

ideogram, ideograph A picture or symbol representing an object or idea without expressing phonetically the sounds of its name—e.g., Egyptian hieroglyphics, Chinese and Japanese characters

IE Internet Explorer. A widely-used web browser for personal computers
http://windows.microsoft.com/en-au/internet-explorer/download-ie

IFCS International Federation of Classification Societies. A group of national, regional and language-based classification societies founded in 1985 to further classification research
http://ifcs.boku.ac.at

IFLA International Federation of Library Associations and Institutions. Organization founded in 1927 to promote international cooperation and development in all fields of library and information service activities
http://www.ifla.org/

IIPA International Intellectual Property Alliance. A coalition of U.S. copyright-based industries, representing book publishing, music, computer software and motion pictures
http://www.iipa.com/

ILL Interlibrary loan. A loan made by one library to another for the use of an individual, including providing a print or electronic copy of the work requested. Cf document delivery

illiteracy The inability to read and write

ILL Protocol *See* ISO ILL Protocol

illuminated Decorated by hand with richly colored ornamental letters, designs, and/or illustrations highlighted in gold or silver. Usually used when describing medieval works—e.g., 'illuminated manuscripts'

illustration A picture, photograph or other visual matter that clarifies, decorates or embellishes a text

illustrator A person who creates visual material to clarify, decorate or embellish text

ILMS Integrated library management system. Also ILS. An automated package of library services that contains several functions such as circulation, cataloging etc.

ILRS Code Australian Interlibrary Resource Sharing Code. A code of practice for interlibrary loan/document delivery, that outlines agreed principles and service level standards
https://www.alia.org.au/resources-and-information/interlibrary-lending/australian-interlibrary-resource-sharing-ilrs-code

ILRS Directory Australian Interlibrary Resource Sharing Directory. A directory of Australian libraries, including library contact details, NUC symbols and interlibrary loan policies, charges etc.
http://www.nla.gov.au/ilrs

ILS Integrated library system. Also ILMS. An automated package of library services that contains several functions such as circulation, cataloging etc.

image retrieval system A system that stores images of documents or pictures in machine-readable form, and enables them to be retrieved via access points such as title and subject

imaging Creating an electronic image of a picture or text by scanning or photographing it

imperfection A printing or binding defect in a book—e.g., some pages missing

import (v) To bring data or files from one computer application or system into another. (n) A publication brought in from another country

impression All copies of an edition of a work printed at one time

imprint Publication details—place, publisher, date of publication

incremental budgeting Financial planning that bids for funds based on the previous year's allocation for particular tasks and expectations of what will be needed in the coming year

incunabula Books printed before 1500

independent librarian A library service provider who works outside a traditional library setting. Cf contracting, outsourcing

index 1. An alphabetical list of terms or topics in a work, usually found at the back. 2. A systematically arranged list that indicates the contents of a document or group of documents

indexer A person who creates back-of-book, database and/or journal indexes

indexing service A periodical publication that regularly and systematically indexes the contents of periodical and sometimes other publications

Indexing Society of Canada / Société canadienne d'indexation ISC/SCI. Canada's national association of professional indexers
http://indexers.ca/

index map A finding aid for a map series. The scale of the index map is small enough to present the entire series on one sheet, which is overlaid by a grid showing the name or number of each map sheet in the series. Cf map index

Index New Zealand INNZ. Online index to New Zealand newspaper and journal articles from the 1950s to the present
http://natlib.govt.nz/collections/a-z/index-new-zealand-innz

indicator In a MARC record, a character that gives additional information about a field—e.g., the first indicator 1 added to the tag 245 shows that a title added entry is to be made

indicator count The number of indicators in each variable data field. In MARC records it is always **2**

informatics The study of the structure, functions, properties, and technology used to record, organize, and disseminate information. Cf information science

information Knowledge in any field, gained by experience or instruction

information agency An organization that provides access to information—e.g., a library, an archive

information broker A person or organization that searches for information on behalf of another person

information commons A concentration of electronic access points adjacent to print resources in an academic library

information desk Also enquiry desk, help desk, readers' adviser's desk, reference desk. The area of a library where staff help people to use the library and answer requests for information

information law 1. The regulation of information by a government regarding censorship, forgery, copyright and intellectual property, freedom of information, intellectual freedom, individual privacy, and computer crime. 2. The branch of legal studies that deals with the regulation of information

information literacy The ability to recognize a need for information, and then to find, organize and use information

information management The planning, budgeting, control and exploitation of the information resources in an organization; including the use of technology to collect, process and use corporate information for efficient management

information orienteering Aligning information strategies to provide a consistent view that values information, enabling it to become a core component of a business strategy

information policy A plan for provision of and access to information in an organization or region

information professional A term including librarians, archivists and records managers, suggesting a broad range of skills and functions

information retrieval Finding information in a library or collection

information science The study of the sources, management, and use of information. Cf informatics

information superhighway A collection of electronic networks that provide access to many databases. Usually refers to the Internet

information technology IT. The acquisition, processing, storage and dissemination of information using computers and telecommunications

information theory The systematic analysis of information, including its nature and flow

Informit Online An online commercial service developed by RMIT Publishing in Australia, providing access by subscription to leading research databases in the Asia Pacific region
http://www.informit.com.au/

Infotrieve An international company that provides, among other services, a commercial document supply service that locates documents and supplies copies for a fee
http://www.infotrieve.com/

IFTA/FIAT International Federation of Television Archives / Fédération Internationale des Archives de Télévision. Set up in 1977 to encourage cooperation among television archives, libraries, and all those engaged in the preservation and exploitation of moving image materials; and to establish international standards for audiovisual media archive management
http://fiatifta.org/

IngentaConnect A commercial alerting and document delivery service in which users pay to order documents online
http://www.ingentaconnect.com/

in-house system An information system established within an institution to meet the needs of its own staff

initial article The word that introduces a noun at the beginning of a title—e.g., the, a, an

initialism A word formed from the initials of the name of an organization, system or service, pronounced letter by letter. Cf acronym

INNZ Index New Zealand. Online index to New Zealand newspaper and journal articles from the 1950s to the present
http://natlib.govt.nz/collections/a-z/index-new-zealand-innz

in press In the process of being printed

in print Available for purchase from the publisher

in process Received but not ready to be used or borrowed because it has not yet been cataloged and end-processed

in-process file A file, manual or automated, of items received by a library and not yet available to users

in progress Used to indicate that a serial or multivolume work is incomplete as further volumes or parts are expected to be published

insert Loose material slipped into a bound publication

inset A smaller picture, map, etc., printed within the border of a larger one

institutional repository An open access digital archive of the intellectual output of an organization, often a university, including journal articles, conference papers, books, theses, course notes, learning objects, sound files and other digital objects created by staff

installment, instalment One part of a work published serially

integrated library management system, integrated library system ILMS, ILS. An automated package of library services that contains several functions such as circulation, cataloging etc.

integrated shelving Also intershelving. All library materials regardless of their format are shelved in one sequence. Cf segregated shelving

integrating resource A resource that is added to or changed by means of updates that do not remain discrete but are integrated into the whole. One of RDA's four modes of issuance. An integrating resource may be tangible (e.g., a loose-leaf manual that is updated by means of replacement pages) or intangible (e.g., a website that is updated either continuously or on a cyclical basis). Cf mode of issuance, finite integrating resource, ongoing integrating resource

intellectual freedom The right of any person to read or express views that may be unpopular or offensive to others

intellectual property IP. Original creative works, which are protected under copyright and patent laws

interlibrary loan ILL. Also interloan (NZ usage). A loan made by one library to another for the use of an individual, including the provision of a photocopy of the original work requested. Cf document delivery

Interlibrary Loan Code for the United States A voluntary code of practice for interlibrary loan/document delivery among libraries in the United States, intended to provide guidelines for loan exchanges between libraries where no other state or consortium agreement applies
http://www.ala.gor/rusa/resources/guidelines/interlibrary

Interlibrary Loan Protocol ISO10160/10161. An international standard for interlibrary loan transactions between libraries and document suppliers

interloan (NZ usage) Also interlibrary loan, ILL. A loan made by one library to another for the use of an individual, including the provision of a photocopy of the original work requested. Cf document delivery

intermediary A person or software program that assists an end-user to select databases, formulate useful queries in correct syntax, and evaluate the relevance of the information retrieved

International Association of Libraries and Museums of the Performing Arts / Société Internationale des Bibliothèques et des Musées des Arts du Spectacle An organization concerned with the documentation of the performing arts, including the development of reference works and cataloging standards
http://www.sibmas.org/

International Association of School Librarianship IASL. Founded to promote school library provision all over the world, includes individual and organizational members
http://www.iasl-online.org/

International Association of Scientific and Technological University Libraries IATUL. An international forum for the exchange of ideas relevant to librarianship in technological universities throughout the world, with membership open to library directors and senior managers
http://www.iatul.org/

International Board on Books for Young People IBBY. An organization to promote global understanding through children's books, comprising national sections working within their own countries to promote children's books
http://www.ibby.org/

International Coalition of Library Consortia ICOLC. An informal group of higher education consortia that serves as an information resource about new technologies, electronic services, pricing, and related issues
http://icolc.net/

International Congress on Medical Librarianship ICML. A conference held every four to five years under the auspices of IFLA, to facilitate the flow of information and ideas in health sciences librarianship

international copyright Copyright protection for works published outside a country, governed by international copyright law and agreements

International Council on Archives / Conseil international des Archives ICA. The professional organization for the world archival community concerned with the preservation, development and use of the world's archival heritage
http://www.ica.org

International Federation of Classification Societies IFCS. A group of national, regional and language-based classification societies founded in 1985 to further classification research
http://ifcs.boku.ac.at/tiki-index.php

International Federation of Film Archives FIAF. An association of the world's leading film archives founded in 1938 to ensure the proper preservation and screening of motion pictures
http://www.fiafnet.org/

International Federation of Library Associations and Institutions IFLA. Organization founded in 1927 to promote international cooperation and development in all fields of library and information service activities
http://www.ifla.org/

International Federation of Television Archives / Fédération Internationale des Archives de Télévision FIAT/IFTA. Set up in 1977 to encourage cooperation among television archives, libraries, and all those engaged in the preservation and exploitation of moving image materials; and to establish international standards for audiovisual media archive management
http://fiatifta.org/

International Indigenous Librarians' Forum An international forum of indigenous librarians from all parts of the world who come together to discuss the information needs and aspirations of their people
http://ailanet.org/activities/international-indigenous-librarians-forum/

International Intellectual Property Alliance IIPA. A coalition of U.S. copyright-based industries, representing book publishing, music, computer software and motion pictures
http://www.iipa.com/

International Literacy Day A day in September established by UNESCO to promote awareness of the value of literacy

International Organization for Standardization ISO. Coordinates major networking standards and seeks international agreement on standards to expand trade, improve quality, increase productivity and lower prices
http://www.iso.org

International Serials Data System ISDS. A network of national centres sponsored by UNESCO, that allocate an ISSN to each serial publication. Cf ISSN, key-title

International Society for Knowledge Organization ISKO. Founded in 1989, an international interdisciplinary society for organization of knowledge, that aims to advance conceptual work in knowledge organization in all forms, such as databases, libraries, dictionaries and the Internet
http://www.isko.org/

International Standard Archival Authority Record for Corporate Bodies, Persons, and Families ISAAR(CPF). The international standard for archival authorities developed by the International Council on Archives in 2004
http://www.ica.org/10203/standards/isaar-cpf-international-standard-archival-authority-record-for-corporate-bodies-persons-and-families-2nd-edition.html

International Standard Bibliographic Description ISBD. Standard set of bibliographic elements in standard order and with standard punctuation, developed to facilitate global exchange of cataloging data. Published by the International Federation of Library Associations and Institutions (IFLA)
http://www.ifla.org/publications/international-standard-bibliographic-description

International Standard Book Number ISBN. A number intended to be unique, assigned by an agency in each country to all books and pamphlets, book readings on cassette, microfiche publications, computer software and multimedia kits containing printed material. Identifies the publisher, language and title. Adopted internationally in 1969

International Standard Identifier for Libraries and Related Organizations ISIL. A standard (ISO 15511:2011) to develop one international code for identifying a library, archive, museum etc., incorporating existing national codes or library symbols, if possible, to minimize impact on already existing systems

International Standard Music Number ISMN. An internationally recognized number assigned to printed music by the International Standard Music Number Agency in Berlin or one of its associated national agencies
http://www.ismn-international.org/

International Standard Serial Number ISSN. An internationally recognized number assigned to each serial publication by the International Serials Data System (ISDS), a network of national centres sponsored by UNESCO
http://www.issn.org/

Internet Explorer IE. A widely-used web browser for personal computers http://windows.microsoft.com/en-au/internet-explorer/download-ie

Internet Protocol IP. The way information is routed through the Internet

Internet Service Provider ISP. An organization that enables a user to connect to the Internet, usually for a fee

internship A period of supervized training in an information agency, linking formal education to real situations

interoperability The ability of computers to communicate with each other using a common set of protocols

intershelving Also integrated shelving. All library materials regardless of their format are shelved in one sequence. Cf segregated shelving

intranet An electronic network within an organization

introduction A preliminary section that introduces a work

inventory 1. Also stocktaking. Checking the items in the collection, including items on loan, awaiting repair etc., against the complete record of a library's holdings (shelflist). 2. Checking library property such as furniture, stationery and equipment against a register to identify missing items. 3. The list itself

inverted heading A heading in which normal word order is transposed, to bring the most significant word to the front—e.g., Cooking, Chinese

inverted title A book title in which the most significant word or phrase is moved to the front in an index—e.g., Middle Ages, History of the

invisible Web Also deep Web. Information on the Web that is not accessible via standard search engines

invoice A document that a dealer sends to a purchaser, itemizing the order and the amount owed

iOS An operating system developed for use on Apple touchscreen mobile devices such as their smartphones and tablet computers. Cf android

IP 1. Intellectual property. Original creative works, which are protected under copyright and patent laws. 2. Internet Protocol. The way information is routed through the Internet

IP address The physical address of a client or server computer attached to a network governed by the TCP/IP protocol, written as four sets of numbers separated by periods—e.g., 201.6.91.47

IRC Internet Relay Chat. Software that allows you to 'chat' to a group of people via the Internet

ISAAR(CPF) International Standard Archival Authority Record for Corporate Bodies, Persons, and Families. The international standard for archival authorities developed by the International Council on Archives in 2004
http://www.ica.org/10203/standards/isaar-cpf-international-standard-archival-authority-record-for-corporate-bodies-persons-and-families-2nd-edition.html

ISAD(G) General International Standard Archival Description. Set of rules for archival description developed by the International Council on Archives in 2000. Cf Encoded Archival Description (EAD), Rules for Archival Description (RAD), Describing Archives: a Content Standard (DACS)
http://www.ica.org/10207/standards/isadg-general-international-standard-archival-description-second-edition.html

ISBD International Standard Bibliographic Description. Standard set of bibliographic elements in standard order and with standard punctuation, developed to facilitate global exchange of cataloging data. Published by the International Federation of Library Associations and Institutions (IFLA)
http://www.ifla.org/publications/international-standard-bibliographic-description

ISBN International Standard Book Number. A number intended to be unique, assigned by an agency in each country to all books and pamphlets, book readings on cassette, microfiche publications, computer software and multimedia kits containing printed material. Identifies the publisher, language and title. Adopted internationally in 1969

ISC/SCI Indexing Society of Canada / Société canadienne d'indexation. Canada's national association of professional indexers
http://indexers.ca/

ISDN Integrated Services Digital Network. Special connections that allow high bandwidth telephone lines to transmit large amounts of data rapidly, using digital instead of analog signals

ISDS International Serials Data System. A network of national centres sponsored by UNESCO, that allocate an ISSN to each serial publication. Cf ISSN, key-title

ISIL International Standard Identifier for Libraries and Related Organizations. A standard (ISO 15511:2011) to develop one international code for identifying a library, archive, museum etc., incorporating existing national codes or library symbols, if possible, to minimize impact on already existing systems

ISKO International Society for Knowledge Organization. Founded in 1989, an international interdisciplinary society for organization of knowledge, that aims to advance conceptual work in knowledge organization in all forms, such as databases, libraries, dictionaries and the Internet
http://www.isko.org/

ISMN International Standard Music Number. An internationally recognized number assigned to printed music by the International Standard Music Number Agency in Berlin or one of its associated National Agencies
http://www.ismn-international.org/

ISO International Organization for Standardization. Coordinates major networking standards and seeks international agreement on standards to expand trade, improve quality, increase productivity and lower prices
http://www.iso.ch/

ISO10160/10161 *See* Interlibrary Loan Protocol

ISO ILL interoperability The ability of computers to communicate with each other using the ISO ILL protocol

ISP Internet Service Provider. An organization that enables a user to connect to the Internet, usually for a fee

ISSN International Standard Serial Number. An internationally recognized number assigned to each serial publication by the International Serials Data System (ISDS), a network of national centres sponsored by UNESCO
http://www.issn.org/

issue (n) A single copy of a serial title. (v) To lend an item

issue date The specific year and/or date, month or season by which a particular issue of a serial is identified—e.g., Spring 2010

issue desk Also charging desk, circulation desk, loans desk. The area of the library where staff handle loans

issue number The number by which a particular issue of a serial is identified—e.g., Issue 46

IT Information technology. The acquisition, processing, storage and dissemination of information by means of computers and telecommunications

item In RDA, a single object with particular characteristics that differentiate it from the rest of the collection in that manifestation—e.g., the specific copy of a publication held by a library, with the library barcode 12345. Cf expression, manifestation, work

jacket Also book jacket, dust cover, dust jacket, dust wrapper, wrapper. Paper cover for a hard-bound book

JACKPHY Japanese, Arabic, Chinese, Korean, Persian, Hindu, Yiddish. Languages not using roman alphabets

jewel case A clear plastic hinged container used to house a CD or DVD

jobber Also book jobber. A wholesale bookseller who supplies books to retailers and libraries. Cf library supplier

joint author Also coauthor. A writer who collaborates with one or more others in preparing a work

joint pseudonym The use of a single pseudonym by two or more authors writing together

Joint Steering Committee for Development of RDA JSC. The committee established to develop and maintain *RDA: Resource Description and Access*. Previously responsible for the maintenance of the *Anglo-American Cataloguing Rules, AACR*
http://www.rda-jsc.org/

joint-use library A library that serves more than one user community—e.g., a joint school and public library. Cf multitype library cooperative

journal 1. A periodical issued by an institution, corporation, or learned society containing current information and reports of activities or works in a particular field. 2. Also diary. A record of events, experiences, thoughts, and observations kept regularly by an individual for personal use

journal circulation list A list of users to whom a journal is to be sent, in the order decided by the library

JPEG graphic Joint Photographic Experts Group graphic. A format widely used to encode and exchange high quality graphics files on the Internet

JSC Joint Steering Committee for Development of RDA. The committee established to develop and maintain *RDA: Resource Description and Access*. Previously responsible for the maintenance of the *Anglo-American Cataloguing Rules, AACR*
http://www.rda-jsc.org/

JSTOR A digital library of backfiles of core academic journals, books and primary sources, mainly available to institutions by subscription but with limited public access to some older public domain content
http://www.jstor.org

juvenile collection A collection of material for children, shelved separately

juvenilia Works produced before an artist or writer reaches maturity

Kate Greenaway Medal An annual award by the (British) Chartered Institute of Library and Information Professionals, instigated in 1956, for outstanding illustration in children's books
http://www.carnegiegreenaway.org.uk/

keeping policy Also holdings policy. A library's policy on the length of time, location, disposal etc. of library material, especially serials

keystone effect The distorted shape of a projected image when the projector is not at right angles to the screen

key-title The unique name given to a serial by the International Serials Data System (ISDS)

keyword A significant term in a document, that identifies subject content

Keyword AAA Thesaurus A whole-of-government thesaurus of administrative function-based terms designed for use by Australian government agencies
http://www.records.nsw.gov.au/recordkeeping/resources/keyword-products/keyword-aaa

keyword in context KWIC. A listing, usually of document titles, with the most significant word in each title arranged in alphabetical order, and with all the other words in the title in their place

Keyword in Series Title KIST. A keyword index to serials held in the British Library

keyword out of context KWOC. A listing of titles with the most significant word in each title arranged in alphabetical order, and with the word by which the list is arranged out of place in the title (often on a separate line)

kick stool A library stool designed to roll along easily but lock in position when someone stands or sits on it

Kindle A popular e-book reader supported by Amazon

KIST Keyword in Series Title. A keyword index to serials held in the British Library

kit An item containing more than one kind of material, none of which is predominant—e.g., a set of slides and an audiocassette

knowledge Understanding gained through study or experience

knowledge management The management practices and supporting technologies in an organization that foster capturing, storing, sharing and using the knowledge of its members; commonly makes use of an intranet http://kmwiki.wikispaces.com/

Koha An open source integrated library management system, originally developed in New Zealand and now widely used by small/special libraries http://koha-community.org/

KWIC Keyword in context. A listing, usually of document titles, with the most significant word in each title arranged in alphabetical order, and with all the other words in the title in their place

KWOC Keyword out of context. A listing of titles with the most significant word in each title arranged in alphabetical order, and with the word by which the list is arranged out of place in the title (often on a separate line)

LA Library Association. *See* Chartered Institute of Library and Information Professionals

LAA Library Association of Australia. *See* Australian Library and Information Association

LAC Library and Archives Canada / Bibliothèque et Archives Canada. The organization established in 2004 combining the holdings, services and staff of the former National Library of Canada and National Archives of Canada http://www.bac-lac.gc.ca

lacuna (Plural lacunae) 1. A gap in a library collection that the library seeks to fill. 2. A missing portion of a manuscript or text

LADD Libraries Australia Document Delivery. The web-based Libraries Australia interface designed for interlibrary lending and document delivery http://www.nla.gov.au/librariesaustralia/services/docdel/

lamination Applying a sheet of plastic to the surface of paper or cardboard by heat or pressure

land The area between the pits on an optical disc such as a CD-ROM

large print Materials that are published in larger than usual print to help people who are visually impaired

La Société bibliographique du Canada *see* Société bibliographique du Canada

law library A special library that specializes in materials for legal studies

layout 1. The style of presentation of a printed publication or online document 2. Preparing copy for typesetting, or for presenting on the screen

LC Library of Congress. The library of the United States Congress; the de facto national library of the United States
http://www.loc.gov/

LCC Library of Congress Classification. A classification scheme developed by the Library of Congress, using numbers and letters. Available in print until 2014 and online as part of the Library's *Classification Web*
http://www.loc.gov/cds/classweb/

LCMARC Library of Congress machine-readable cataloging format. Changed name to USMARC in the 1980s and was harmonized with Canadian MARC to create MARC 21 in the late 1990s

LCNA Library of Congress Name Authorities *See* Library of Congress Authorities

LC-PCC PS Library of Congress-Program for Cooperative Cataloging Policy Statements. Also Library of Congress Policy Statements. The Library's policy decisions on how it will implement or interpret specific aspects of the RDA cataloging guidelines. Replaces *Library of Congress Rule Interpretations*, an equivalent publication dealing with AACR cataloging practices
http://access.rdatoolkit.org/

LCSH Library of Congress Subject Headings. The authoritative list of subject headings compiled and maintained by the Library of Congress. Available in print until 2014 and online as part of the Library's *Classification Web* http://www.loc.gov/aba/cataloging/subject/

leader Top line of a MARC record that gives information about the record to the computer program that processes it

lead-in vocabulary Cross-references in a subject thesaurus that direct the user from related terms to a designated subject heading

leaf A sheet of paper consisting of two pages, one on each side

leaflet An unbound publication of two to four pages

learning hub A facility in a school or college library incorporating individual and interactive study, research and collaborative areas as well as spaces for group work, integrated with wi-fi Internet access, printing and scanning services and other technology

learning resources centre Also media centre. A facility in a school or college that holds media equipment, with staff to assist students and instructors in using it

legacy data Existing catalog records that were created using older cataloging conventions like AACR2. These are the library's 'legacy' of information

legal deposit The law that obliges publishers to deposit copies of their publications in libraries in the country in which they are published, including the national library and other libraries designated in the Act

Legal Deposit Libraries Shared Cataloguing Programme A program managed by the British Library to share responsibility for cataloging new legal deposit publications among the six British and Irish legal deposit libraries http://www.bl.uk/bibliographic/clscp.html

legend A visual aid that explains the symbols used in an atlas or on a map

legislative library A library that provides materials and services to support the work of a state or provincial legislature. Cf parliamentary library

legislative reference service A government agency—e.g., Congressional Research Services (U.S.), the Parliamentary Research Branch (Canada)—that provides research assistance to legislatures and other government agencies

lending right *See* educational lending right, public lending right

lenticular screen Type of screen made of beads that reflects images very effectively with limited light. Lenticular screen technology is being used to try to develop 3D TV and film images that will not require 3D glasses

letter-by-letter alphabetization Arranging in strict alphabetical order ignoring word breaks—e.g., Newbery before New England. Cf word-by-word alphabetization

level of description In AACR2, the amount of detail in a bibliographic record. AACR2 had three levels of description, from basic to very detailed records

lexicography Creating a dictionary or glossary

lexicology The study of the origins, form, and meaning of words

lexicon A dictionary, most often of ancient languages

LexisNexis An international company providing, among others, an online legal, news and business information service that gives access to case law and legislation from the major Commonwealth countries, U.S. and Asia
http://www.lexisnexis.com

LIANZA Library and Information Association of New Zealand Aoteroa / Te Rau Herenga o Aotearoa. The professional body in New Zealand for those engaged in librarianship and information management. See their website for their interest groups, publications, awards and prizes
http://www.lianza.org.nz

LibDex A user-generated worldwide directory of library homepages, their web-based OPACs, and their Friends of the Library pages
http://www.libdex.com/

LIBER Ligue des Bibliothèques Européennes de Recherche / Association of European Research Libraries. The principal association of the major research libraries of Europe, founded under the auspices of the Council of Europe
http://libereurope.eu/

LibGuides 1. A guide to the resources of a particular subject area, developed by library staff and usually held by their library. Cf topic guide, pathfinder.
2. Brand name for a customizable template used by reader education staff to develop library guides, developed by Springshare. Cf Springshare

librarian A person with a library qualification recognized as professional by the relevant library association, or performing work at a professional level

librarianship 1. The profession of the people who staff libraries, and the management of libraries and library services. 2. The professional knowledge and skill with which recorded information is selected, acquired, organized, stored, maintained, retrieved, and disseminated to meet the needs of clients

Libraries Australia A resource sharing service coordinated by the National Library of Australia for Australian libraries and their users. Used for reference, collection development, cataloging and interlibrary lending; based on the Australian National Bibliographic Database (ANBD)
http://www.nla.gov.au/librariesaustralia/

Libraries Australia Cataloguing Client The Libraries Australia software that allows direct, real-time input and editing of bibliographic and authority records in the Australian National Bibliographic Database (ANBD)
http://www.nla.gov.au/librariesaustralia/services/cataloguing/client/

Libraries Australia Document Delivery LADD. The web-based Libraries Australia interface designed for interlibrary lending and document delivery
http://www.nla.gov.au/librariesaustralia/services/docdel/

Libraries Australia Search The web-based Libraries Australia search interface designed for bibliographic searching, locating items and simple cataloging
http://www.nla.gov.au/librariesaustralia/services/search/

library 1. A collection of books and other materials for reading, study or reference. 2. A place housing a collection of materials for reading, study or reference, or from which to borrow

library administration 1. Managing a library, including budgeting, policy-making, personnel management, and program assessment. 2. Persons responsible for library management, usually the chief librarian and his or her immediate staff

Library and Archives Canada / Bibliothèque et Archives Canada LAC. The national organization established in 2004 combining the holdings, services and staff of the former National Library of Canada and National Archives of Canada
http://www.bac-lac.gc.ca/

Library and Information Association of New Zealand Aoteroa / Te Rau Herenga o Aotearoa LIANZA. The professional body in Aotearoa New Zealand for those engaged in librarianship and information management. See their website for their interest groups, publications, awards and prizes http://www.lianza.org.nz

Library and Information Science Abstracts LISA. An online international database of abstracts and citations for library professionals and other information specialists. Available on subscription via ProQuest http://proquest.libguides.com/lisa

Library Association *See* Chartered Institute of Library and Information Professionals

Library Association of Australia *See* Australian Library and Information Association

Library Bill of Rights An affirmation by the American Library Association that all libraries are forums for information and ideas, and that they should embody the principles of free expression, free access and non-discrimination. Cf School Library Bill of Rights

library binding A durable form of binding

library board An advisory committee attached to a public or academic library, representing its primary user group(s), e.g., taxpayers or university members

library card Also borrower's card. A paper or plastic card that shows a registered borrower is entitled to check out materials from a library

library collection The sum of books and materials owned by a library

library consortium A group of libraries joined by formal or informal agreement to achieve a specific purpose—e.g., to share the cost and use of a library management system. The consortium is often empowered to represent its members as a legal entity. Cf library network

library culture The values informing a particular library or library system

library director (primarily American usage) The person responsible for the operations of a library, also variously titled Director-General, Chief Librarian, Librarian-in-Charge, Principal Librarian, etc.

library district 1. In the USA, an area in which the citizens vote to accept a local tax in support of a public library. 2. In Canada, one of the areas into which a state or province is divided in order to administer its libraries

library education 1. Teaching programs leading to a professional or paraprofessional qualification in library science. 2. Also bibliographic instruction, client education, library orientation, reader education, reader instruction, user education. Helping people to derive the most benefit from using a library

library extension activities Activities aimed at people who do not have access to a library—e.g., storytelling to children

Library Literature & Information Science An online index to the literature of library science, produced by H.W. Wilson and available as both an index and full-text service via Ebsco Publishing
http://www.ebscohost.com/wilson

library management system LMS. Also integrated library management system, integrated library system. An automated package of library services that contains several functions such as circulation, cataloging etc.

library network Two or more libraries that share resources or exchange information. Cf library consortium, library system

Library of Congress The library of the United States Congress; the de facto national library of the United States
http://www.loc.gov/

Library of Congress Authorities Online source of authorized subject, name, title and name/title headings, available free of charge
http://authorities.loc.gov/

Library of Congress Classification LCC. A classification scheme developed by the Library of Congress, using numbers and letters. Available in print until 2014 and online as part of the Library's *Classification Web*
http://www.loc.gov/cds/classweb/

Library of Congress Name Authorities *See* Library of Congress Authorities

Library of Congress Policy Statements, Also Library of Congress-Program for Cooperative Cataloging Policy Statements LC-PCC PS. The Library's policy decisions on how it will implement or interpret specific aspects of the RDA cataloging guidelines. Replaces *Library of Congress Rule Interpretations*, an equivalent publication dealing with AACR cataloging practices
http://access.rdatoolkit.org/

Library of Congress-Program for Cooperative Cataloging Policy Statements Also Library of Congress Policy Statements LC-PCC PS. The Library's policy decisions on how it will implement or interpret specific aspects of the RDA cataloging guidelines. Replaces *Library of Congress Rule Interpretations*, an equivalent publication dealing with AACR cataloging practices http://access.rdatoolkit.org/

Library of Congress Subject Authorities *See* Library of Congress Authorities

Library of Congress Subject Headings LCSH. The authoritative list of subject headings compiled and maintained by the Library of Congress. Available in print until 2014 and online as part of the Library's *Classification Web* http://www.loc.gov/aba/cataloging/subject/

library officer Designation for a library paraprofessional, used in some countries for those with less training than a library technician and in other countries as a synonymous term. Cf library technician

library orientation Also bibliographic instruction, client education, reader education, reader instruction, user education. Helping people to derive the most benefit from using the library

library school A school or department granting degrees and/or diplomas that are recognized qualifications for professional positions in libraries or related institutions

library science Also librarianship. The professional knowledge and skill with which recorded information is selected, acquired, organized, stored, maintained, retrieved, and disseminated to meet the needs of clients

library supplier A company whose primary function is to obtain material from publishers and supply it to libraries. Cf jobber, book jobber

library survey 1. A method of collecting data to determine how well a library is meeting the needs of its users and the library's objectives. 2. The report resulting from such a study

library symbol A standardized, shorthand way to identify libraries, used in interlibrary lending and union listings. Often composed of groups of letters, the first indicating the state or territory of the library, the others the institution itself. DOCLINE IDs, NUC and OCLC symbols are examples of library symbols. Cf NUC symbol, International Standard Identifier for Libraries

library system A group of libraries administered in common, such as a central library and its branches. Cf library network

library technician 1. A person with a qualification in librarianship recognized as paraprofessional by the relevant library association, or performing work at a paraprofessional level. Cf library officer. 2. (PNG) Designation introduced in 1982 to encompass the duties of library assistant and library officer

library trustee A member of a board that oversees the work and administration of a library

licensing agreement A contract between a library and a supplier to lease databases or other resources under specific conditions for a stated period on payment of a fee

Ligue des Bibliothèques Européennes de Recherche / Association of European Research Libraries LIBER. The principal association of the major research libraries of Europe, founded under the auspices of the Council of Europe http://libereurope.eu/

lilliput edition Also miniature edition. An edition in which the copies are three inches or less in height and width, printed in very small typeface

limited edition An edition in which a restricted number of copies is printed, often more expensively produced than a regular edition

line-item budget A budget in which anticipated expenditures are divided into general categories (salaries and wages, materials, equipment, etc.) for the purpose of planning the allocation of resources and tracking expenditures

link 1. Also hyperlink. A keyword, phrase or graphic on the Web that connects to another web page. 2. A connection between two files or data items so that a change in one is reflected by a change in the second

link rot The tendency for links and bookmarks to point to web pages that have moved or been deleted

Linux A popular, open source version of the Unix operating system that is widely used for servers and personal computing devices www.linux.org; www.linux.org.au; www.linux.com

LISA Library and Information Science Abstracts. An online international database of abstracts and citations for library professionals and other information specialists. Available on subscription via ProQuest http://proquest.libguides.com/lisa

list price Also published price. The publisher's advertised, undiscounted price

list server The software responsible for the management and distribution of mailing lists. A list server automatically distributes an email message from one member of a list to all other members on that list

literacy The ability to read and write

Literacy Week A week of activities to promote an awareness of the value of literacy, celebrated in the week of International Literacy Day, September 8

literary warrant The volume of books written, or likely to be written, on a topic

literary work A work, other than a sacred work, written in a literary form—e.g., a poem, drama, novel etc.—and regarded as being of high quality

literature 1. Writings of outstanding literary quality. 2. Writings in a particular language or period. 3. The body of writings by scholars in a particular field

literature review A survey of written scholarship in a specific field

literature search A systematic and thorough search for information on a topic

LMS Library management system. Also integrated library management system, integrated library system. An automated package of library services that contains several functions such as circulation, cataloging etc.

loan A recorded transaction in which a borrower removes an item from a collection for a stated period of time

loan period Also borrowing period, checkout period. The time for which an item in a library may be checked out by a borrower

loans desk Also charging desk, circulation desk, issue desk. The area of the library where staff handle loans

local collection Also local history collection, local studies collection. A library's books and other material relating to a specific geographical area, usually the locality of the library

local subdivision Also geographic subdivision. The subdivision of a class or subject heading by place (region, country, state, city, etc.)

location Where an item is housed. This can be the name of the library or the part of a collection

location symbol A symbol showing the collection in which an item belongs — e.g., F for fiction

loc. cit. Abbreviation for Latin *loco citato* (in the place cited). Used in a footnote to avoid repeating the title of the work already cited. Use of *op. cit.* is increasingly preferred

logical record length The length of a self-contained MARC record

long-playing record LP. A phonograph record that is played at 33rpm

loose-leaf filing Keeping a publication up-to-date by inserting new pages and removing old ones according to instructions from the publisher

loose-leaf publication A serial publication in a binder, that is kept up-to-date by inserting new pages and removing old ones according to instructions from the publisher

lower-case Small letter (e.g., a, b, c). Cf upper-case

LP Long-playing record. A phonograph record that is played at 33rpm

machine-aided indexing Automated indexing without human intervention

machine-readable Needing a computer to process or interpret

MAchine Readable Cataloging MARC. A system developed by the Library of Congress in the 1960s so that libraries can share machine-readable bibliographic data. The MARC data elements are the foundation of many library catalogs. Cf MARC 21, UNIMARC

magazine 1. A popular serial. 2. A holder for slides to be shown using a slide projector. Can also be used to store slides

magnetic tape A plastic tape coated with iron oxide, used to record sound, images and/or digital data by magnetizing and demagnetizing the particles of iron oxide

main entry In AACR2, the principal entry in a catalog, that contains the complete record of a resource. Cf added entry

main heading The first part of a composite heading that includes a subheading—e.g., in the heading 'Mentoring—Australia', 'Mentoring' is the main heading

main library Also central library. The headquarters of a library system, where management decisions are made, and the main collection held

malware MALicious softWARE. Software designed to disrupt computer operations or gain access to personal computers. It includes viruses, worms, spyware, trojans and logic bombs

Man Booker Prize for Fiction An annual prize for the best novel in English by a citizen of the British Commonwealth or Ireland and published in the U.K. http://www.themanbookerprize.com/

manga A style of Japanese comic books and graphic novels, usually serialized and typically aimed at adults as well as children. Cf graphic novel

manifestation In RDA, one of the Group 1 entities described in *Functional Requirements for Bibliographic Records* as the physical embodiment of the expression of a work. Cf expression, item, work

manual (adj) Without the use of a computer. (n) A book of instruction on doing, making or performing something

manual indexing Content analysis and indexing done by people

manufacture statement In RDA, a statement identifying: the place or places of manufacture; manufacturer or manufacturers; and date or dates of manufacture of a resource in a published form

manuscript MS. A handwritten or typescript document

Maori Subject Headings / Ngā Ūpoko Tukutuku A thesaurus of Maori terms for use in New Zealand public and academic libraries http://mshupoko.natlib.govt.nz

map A representation, normally to scale, of an area of the earth's surface or another celestial body

map index An alphabetical list of place names from a map or atlas, giving the location of each feature. Cf index map

map library A library that collects mainly maps, atlases, and related cartographic material

MARC MAchine Readable Cataloging. A format developed by the Library of Congress in 1966 so that libraries can share machine-readable bibliographic data. The MARC data elements are the foundation of many library catalogs. Cf MARC 21, UNIMARC

MARC 21 The harmonization of USMARC and CANMARC, and increasingly the international standard for representing and communicating bibliographic and related information in machine-readable form; maintained by the Library of Congress in consultation with various user communities. Cf UNIMARC
http://www.loc.gov/marc/

MARCit A service provided by Ex Libris that catalogs websites and other electronic resources as MARC records
http://www.exlibrisgroup.com/category/SFXMARCit!

marginalia Writing in the margins of manuscripts

mark of omission Punctuation mark of three dots (…), indicating something has been left out

mashup A web page or web application that uses data from more than one source to create a new service, displayed with a unique look in a single graphic interface—e.g., combining the addresses and photos of a library's branches with a map

masthead Statement of title, ownership, editors etc. of a newspaper or serial

material specific details In AACR2, details of bibliographic description that are specific to a particular type of material—e.g., the scale of a map, the numbering of a serial

mathematical data Information for maps including statements of scale, projection, coordinates and equinox

media 1. Material in all formats that communicate information. 2. Audiovisual materials such as films, slides, videorecordings, compact discs, audiotapes, and computer software

media centre Also learning resources centre. A facility in a school or college that holds media equipment, with staff to assist students and instructors in using it

media monitoring Also press clipping service. A service that examines the press, radio and television regularly for information on specific topics, and reports to requesting clients

mediated search A search in which a reference librarian helps clients to find the information they need, usually using electronic databases

media type In RDA, the type of device needed to view, play or run the resource—e.g., audio, video, computer, unmediated (for print material) etc.

medical library A special library that serves the needs of students, researchers, and practitioners in the health sciences

Medical Library Association MLA. U.S. organization that supports health sciences library and information professionals in enhancing the quality of health care, education, and research
http://www.mlanet.org/

medium (Plural media) The physical material on which data are recorded—e.g., paper, film, magnetic tape or disc, optical disc

MEDLINE The U.S. National Library of Medicine's bibliographic database of journal citations and abstracts for biomedical literature from around the world, accessed through PubMed and PubMed Central. Cf PubMed
http://www.nlm.nih.gov/bsd

memoir A record of events written from personal observation

memory stick Also flash drive, USB flash drive, thumb drive. A small removable and rewritable data storage device that plugs into a USB port, used for storage, backup and transfer of computer files. Often used in preference to CD-ROMs because of its high storage capacity, small size, durability and reliability. Cf CD-ROM

mending Minor book repairs, not requiring the replacement of any material

mentoring Informal guidance and encouragement from a more experienced worker

merge (n) A program for joining different lists, databases, etc. (v) To come together—e.g., when two serials join to become one new title

MeSH Medical Subject Headings, maintained by the U.S. National Library of Medicine, and used for indexing articles, cataloging books and other holdings, and searching MeSH-indexed databases, including MEDLINE
http://www.nlm.nih.gov/mesh

metadata Descriptive information used to describe and provide access to information resources, especially Internet sites and documents

Metadata Object Description Schema MODS. A metadata format for bibliographic material, including some elements from MARC21 and intended to complement other metadata formats. Developed in 2002 and maintained by the Library of Congress

meta-index An index of indexes

meta search engine A service that passes a query on to a number of other search engines, and then combines the results. Cf federated search

MHz MegaHertz. A measurement of radio frequency, used to indicate the processing speed of a computer

microfiche Also fiche. A microfilmed transparency about the size and shape of a filing card, that may have on it many pages of print

microfilm 16mm or 35mm film containing a sequence of microphotographs

microform All forms of micro reduction on film or paper. Includes microfilm, microfiche, micro-opaques (now rare) and aperture cards

micro-opaque A copy of part or all of a document micro-reduced in size by photographic means and printed on a card

Miles Franklin Literary Award An annual award for a published novel portraying Australian life in any of its phases
http://www.milesfranklin.com.au/

Millennium A large integrated library management system, developed and marketed by Innovative Interfaces
http://www.iii.com/products/millennium

miniature edition Also lilliput edition. An edition in which the copies are three inches or less in height and width, printed in very small typeface

minicomputer A medium-sized computer, able to serve several hundred users, often used to run a library's online catalog

mirror site A copy of a website that contains the same information as the original, located in a different place on the Internet for backup and/or to provide access from a different geographical region

mixed notation A combination of types of symbol—e.g., numbers and letters used in Library of Congress Classification. Cf pure notation

mixed responsibility Also multiple statements of responsibility. Different persons or bodies make different kinds of contributions to a work—e.g., author and illustrator. Cf shared responsibility

MLA Medical Library Association. U.S. organization that supports health sciences library and information professionals in enhancing the quality of health care, education, and research
http://www.mlanet.org/

MLA Music Library Association. Professional U.S. organization devoted to music librarianship
http://www.musiclibraryassoc.org/

MLA style A bibliographic format for citing information based on the requirements of the Modern Language Association. Cf electronic style, APA style, Chicago style
http://www.mla.org/style

mnemonic Pronounced 'nemonic'. Aiding memory

mobile app A small computer program (i.e. 'application') designed to be downloaded by a user to run on smartphones, tablet computers and other mobile devices. Cf app

mobile library A collection of library materials able to be transported to various locations to provide a library service

mode of issuance In RDA, a categorization reflecting whether a resource is issued in one or more parts, the way it is updated, and its intended termination. RDA recognizes four modes of issuance: single unit, multipart monograph, serial, and integrating resource

modification Alteration of a work

MODS Metadata Object Description Schema. A metadata format for bibliographic material, including some elements from MARC21 and intended to complement other metadata formats. Developed in 2002 and maintained by the Library of Congress

module Part of an automated system that can perform on its own, or within the larger system—e.g., a serials control module

mono, monaural Also monophonic. Using one channel for transmitting sound. Cf stereophonic

monochrome plate An illustration printed in one color

monograph A publication either complete in one part or in a finite number of separate parts. Cf serial

monographic series A series of related monographs with a collective title as well as individual titles

monograph in series A resource with its own title proper, that is part of a series with a common series title

monophonic Also mono, monaural. Using one channel for transmitting sound. Cf stereo, stereophonic

Montana New Zealand Book Awards. *See* New Zealand Post Book Awards

monthly Issued once a month

morgue Also newspaper library. A library in the office of a newspaper, containing back issues and reference material used by staff members to prepare their articles

motion picture A length of film from which a sequence of still photographs can be projected to give the illusion of continuous motion

Moys Classification A specialized classification scheme for law devised by Betty Moys, incorporating aspects of the Library of Congress and Dewey classification schemes
http://special-cataloguing.com/node/1429

Mozilla A community of developers using an open source toolkit, creators of Linux, Firefox browser and other products
http://www.mozilla.com

mp3 player A device that stores and plays digital audio files like songs and spoken word (audio) books. Cf playaway

MS Manuscript. A handwritten or typescript document

multicast To transmit text, audio or video simultaneously to specified groups of users on a network

multimedia 1. Computer-based presentation of information using more than one medium—e.g., text, graphics, sound—and emphasising interactivity. 2. In cataloging, containing more than one category of material, no one of which is predominant

multipart monograph A resource issued in two or more parts (either simultaneously or successively) that is complete or intended to be completed within a finite number of parts (e.g., a dictionary in two volumes, three audiocassettes issued as a set). One of RDA's four modes of issuance. Cf mode of issuance

multiple access Having more than one access point to a file—e.g., a computer file of bibliographic records accessible by author, title, subject, and keyword(s)

multiple statements of responsibility Also mixed responsibility. Different persons or bodies make different kinds of contributions to a work—e.g., author and illustrator. Cf single statement of responsibility, statement of responsibility

multitasking 1. The capacity of a computer to use more than one application to perform more than one task at one time. 2. The ability of a person to deal with two or more tasks simultaneously

multitype library cooperative Two or more types of libraries working together to provide library and information services. Cf joint-use library

museum library A special library maintained by a museum, that contains material related to its exhibits

musical presentation statement In AACR2, a term or phrase indicating the physical presentation of the music—e.g., score, miniature score. RDA uses the term 'format of notated music'

Music Australia An online service that provided access to music scores, sound recordings, websites and other music-related material held by many Australian cultural institutions. Now integrated into Trove

music library A special library that collects mainly music scores, recorded music, and material about music and musicians

Music Library Association MLA. Professional U.S. organization devoted to music librarianship
http://www.musiclibraryassoc.org/

mylar plastic Strong, non-acidic plastic used in library materials and coverings

NAA National Archives of Australia. Formerly Australian Archives. The organization responsible for ensuring that Commonwealth government records are identified, preserved and made available to researchers
http://www.naa.gov.au

NACO Name Authority Cooperative Program. The name authority component of the Program for Cooperative Cataloging of the Library of Congress
http://www.loc.gov/aba/pcc/naco

NAL National Agricultural Library. One of four National Libraries in the United States, the Library is part of the Agricultural Research Service of the U.S. Department of Agriculture
http://www.nal.usda.gov/

Name Authority Cooperative Program NACO. The name authority component of the Program for Cooperative Cataloging of the Library of Congress
http://www.loc.gov/aba/pcc/naco

name authority file A collection of authority records containing the preferred forms of headings for names, including personal and corporate names. It can be on cards, microfiche, CD-ROM or online

named revision A named reissue of a particular edition containing changes from that edition

name-title added entry An added entry under the combined name of a person, family or corporate body and the title of a resource—e.g., Dickens, Charles, 1812-1870. A Christmas carol

NARA National Archives and Records Administration. The federal agency responsible for managing all U.S. federal records
http://www.archives.gov/

narrower term NT. A more specific subject heading. Cf broader term, related term

National Agricultural Library NAL. One of four National Libraries in the United States, the Library is part of the Agricultural Research Service of the U.S. Department of Agriculture
http://www.nal.usda.gov/

National and State Libraries Australasia NSLA. A group comprising the national libraries of Australia and New Zealand, and the State and Territory libraries of Australia. NSLA members work collaboratively to strengthen the information infrastructure, work on joint projects, and provide a single voice to governments and stakeholders on library and information issues
http://www.nsla.org.au/

National Archives and Library of Kiribati A division of the Republic of Kiribati Ministry of Education. The archives are a collection of current and historical publications and other records of Kiribati. The library is responsible for library and information services in Kiribati
http://moe.gov.ki/divisions/knla/

National Archives and Library, Tuvalu The collection of current and historical publications and other records of Tuvalu

National Archives and Public Records Service of Papua New Guinea The division of the Office of Libraries and Archives concerned with preserving archival materials and records for the nation. Cf National Library Service of Papua New Guinea
http://www.parbica.org/sharing/publications/other-publications/naprs-png.aspx

National Archives and Records Administration NARA. The federal agency responsible for managing all U.S. federal records
http://www.archives.gov/

National Archives of Australia NAA. The organization responsible for ensuring that Commonwealth government records are identified, preserved and made available to researchers
http://www.naa.gov.au

National Archives of Canada *See* Library and Archive Canada

National Archives of Fiji The collection of records of the British Colonial Administration in Fiji, the government of Fiji and some private records. Contains the Sir Alport Barker Memorial Library, which, together with the University of the South Pacific Library, is the library for legal deposit in Fiji
http://www.archives.gov.fj/

National Archives of New Zealand *See* Archives New Zealand

National Bibliographic Database 1. *See* Australian National Bibliographic Database. 2. (NZ) A database of bibliographic records with holdings of New Zealand libraries, and of records without holdings from the British National Bibliography, the Library of Congress and the National Library of Australia

national bibliography A listing of the publications of a country, about that country, by the residents of that country, in the language of that country

national biography 1. A publication containing biographical information about notable people in or associated with a particular country. 2. The branch of biography concerned with the lives of important people in or associated with a country

National Book Foundation, National Book Awards Established in 1989 to promote appreciation of exceptional American literature, the Foundation administers and sponsors annual National Book Awards
http://www.nationalbook.org/

National Book Month A month of activities to increase interest in books and reading, celebrated in the U.S. in October

National Book Week (Australia). *See* National Literacy and Numeracy Week

National Endowment for the Humanities. A U.S. government-funded agency that promotes knowledge of human history, thought and culture by providing grants for humanities projects, including support for library programs
http://www.neh.gov

National Film and Sound Archive The Australian national collection of motion pictures and sound recordings, housed in Canberra
http://www.nfsa.gov.au/

National Information Center for Educational Media NICEM. An organization that maintains a major bibliographic database of educational audiovisual materials, accessed by subscription
http://www.nicem.com/

National Information Standards Organization NISO. Subordinate body of the American National Standards Institute, which generates key standards in information management
http://www.niso.org

national library A library maintained by government funds and serving the nation as whole. It is usually the country's legal deposit library, and collects and preserves the nation's literature

National Library of Australia NLA. The Commonwealth-funded library responsible for ensuring that all Australians have access to information, and assisting all other Australian libraries through the Distributed National Collection and a wide range of support services
http://www.nla.gov.au

National Library of Australia Policy Statements NLA PS. A series of statements, arranged in RDA instruction number order, recording the Library's policy decisions on how it will implement or interpret specific aspects of the RDA cataloging guidelines. Available via the 'Resources' tab of the RDA Toolkit
http://access.rdatoolkit.org/

National Library of Canada *See* Library and Archives Canada

National Library of Education NLE. One of four national libraries in the U.S., and the library of the U.S. Department of Education. Maintained as part of the Institute of Education Science's National Center for Education Evaluation and Regional Assistance
http://ies.ed.gov/ncee/projects/nle

National Library of Kiribati *See* National Archives and Library of Kiribati

National Library of Medicine NLM. One of four national libraries in the United States, and the world's largest biomedical library, it covers subjects from medical history to biotechnology
http://www.nlm.nih.gov

National Library of New Zealand / Te Puna Mātauranga o Aoteoroa The government-funded cultural and information centre whose role is to collect and maintain literature and resources that relate to New Zealand and the Pacific, to make this information readily available, and to preserve New Zealand's documentary heritage for future generations
http://www.natlib.govt.nz

National Library of South Africa A library and information centre of excellence in Africa, and the custodian of South Africa's key knowledge resources and documentary heritage
http://www.nlsa.ac.za

National Library of the Cook Islands The library that maintains the national and public lending collections of the Cook Islands

National Library Service of Papua New Guinea The division of the Office of Libraries and Archives concerned with developing the national collection, promoting literacy and coordinating library services. Cf National Archives and Public Records Service of Papua New Guinea

National Library Service of the Solomon Islands *See* Solomon Islands National Library Service

National Library Society / Te Ropu Tautoko I Te Puna Matauranga A society formed to strengthen the links between the National Library of New Zealand and the community, and to support the National Library to achieve its goals
http://nationallibrarysociety.org.nz/

National Library Week In the U.S., a week of celebrating the contributions of libraries, librarians and library workers and promoting library use and support, sponsored by the American Library Association
http://www.ala.org/news/mediapresscenter/factsheets/nationallibraryweek

National Literacy and Numeracy Week A week of activities in Australia to increase interest in books and reading—celebrated in the first week of August

National Science Library / Bibliothèque scientifique nationale The library of the National Research Council Canada, providing information and services to support Canadian discovery, innovation and commercialization activities
http://www.nrc-cnrc.gc.ca/eng/publications/library

National Technical Information Service NTIS. U.S. Government organization that sells scientific and technical publications published by or associated with the U.S. government
http://www.ntis.gov

national union catalog, national union catalogue A listing of the holdings of a large number of libraries in a particular country

National Union Catalog NUC. A record of older publications held in libraries in the United States and Canada, many of which do not appear in electronic databases. It is available in print and on microfiche
http://www.loc.gov/rr/main/inforeas/union.html

National Union Catalogue NUC. In Australia, originally a card-based catalog of the holdings of Australian libraries. Now incorporated into Libraries Australia

National Union Catalogue symbol NUC symbol. The Australian library symbol that is a unique identifier for an organization that contributes bibliographic records to the Australian National Bibliographic Database. NUC symbols are used in Libraries Australia Document Delivery (LADD) to indicate libraries' holdings for interlibrary loan purposes

natural language 1. Terms used in a document or subject heading without being modified or inverted. 2. Computer programming language that resembles human language

NCIP NISO Circulation Interchange Protocol = Z39.83. A standard to facilitate communication between circulation and interlibrary loan systems

n.d. No date, used in AACR2 bibliographic records to indicate the publication date is unknown. RDA uses the phrase 'date of publication not identified'

Nelson Memorial Public Library The main library in Samoa; it acts as a national library

nesting Grouping search terms so that a sequence of searches can be performed – e.g., '(women or girls) and physical fitness' searches for either 'women' or 'girls' and combines the result of that search with the term 'physical fitness'

net 1. Also net published price. Terms in which a publisher specifies that a book must be sold with no discount. 2. The Internet

network 1. A group of computers connected together to transmit information to each other. 2. *See* library network

Newark loan system A manual circulation system that uses a book card and a borrower card. The book card has the borrower's name or number and the date due entered on it. It is filed in date due order and subfiled by call number

Newbery Medal An annual award made by the American Library Association's Association for Library Service to Children, to the author of the most distinguished contribution to American children's literature
http://www.ala.org/alsc/awardsgrants/bookmedia/newberymedal/newberymedal

newsgroup Also discussion group. A group communicating on the Internet that can form on any topic or subject. Messages (news) can be sent electronically to the group to read and comment on

newsletter A serial publication consisting of a few pages of news and information for members of an organization or interest group

newspaper A printed publication issued regularly, usually daily or weekly, containing news, comment, features and advertising

newspaper cutting An article cut from a newspaper. Usually filed in a vertical file or photocopied and sent to identified library users

newspaper library Also morgue. A library in the office of a newspaper, containing back issues and reference material used by staff members to prepare their articles

newsprint Paper on which newspapers are printed. Contains a high proportion of ground wood pulp that causes the paper to become yellow and brittle over time

news summary A weekly or monthly looseleaf digest of news events, designed for storage in binders in chronological order

New Zealand Book Council / Te Kaunihera Pukapuka O Aotearoa An independent, non-profit body established in 1972 to promote and celebrate the love of books and reading
http://www.bookcouncil.org.nz/

New Zealand Books in Print *See* Global Books in Print

New Zealand Children's Book Foundation *See* Storylines Children's Literature Foundation and Storylines Trust

New Zealand Government Online NZGO. A website that provides an overview of New Zealand and its government, access to government services information, and government agency contact details
http://www.govt.nz

New Zealand Interlibrary Loan System, New Zealand Interloan Scheme New Zealand member libraries provide loans and copies of articles to other member libraries, using the Te Puna Interloan ILL management system
http://www.lianza.org.nz/about/profile/interloan/interloan_handbook.html

New Zealand Library and Information Association NZLIA. *See* Library and Information Association of New Zealand

New Zealand National Bibliography NZNB. Monthly listing of i published in or about New Zealand and added to *Publications New Zealand*, the online national bibliography. NZNB is available in Word, Excel and PDF formats. Cf Publications New Zealand
http://natlib.govt.nz/librarians/national-library-services/publications-new-zealand

New Zealand National Register of Archives and Manuscripts / Te Rarangi Puranga, Tuhinga Ake o te Motu *See* The Community Archive

New Zealand Post Book Awards Formerly Montana New Zealand Book Awards. National awards for poetry, fiction, illustrated and general non-fiction, picture books and junior fiction, celebrating excellence in books written by New Zealanders
http://www.booksellers.co.nz/awards/new-zealand-post-book-awards

Ngā Taonga Kōrero / Sound Archives New Zealand's foremost radio archive, responsible for managing, collecting, preserving and providing access to the nation's recorded radio heritage
http://www.soundarchives.co.nz/

Ngā Ūpoko Tukutuku / Maori Subject Headings A thesaurus of Maori terms for use in New Zealand public and academic libraries
http://mshupoko.natlib.govt.nz

NICEM National Information Center for Educational Media. An organization that maintains a major bibliographic database of educational audiovisual materials, accessed by subscription
http://www.nicem.com/

NISO National Information Standards Organization. Subordinate body of the American National Standards Institute that generates key standards in information management
http://www.niso.org

NLA National Library of Australia. The government-funded library responsible for ensuring that all Australians have access to information, and assisting all other Australian libraries through the Distributed National Collection and a wide range of support services
http://www.nla.gov.au

NLA PS National Library of Australia Policy Statements. A series of statements, arranged in RDA instruction number order, recording the Library's policy decisions on how it will implement or interpret specific aspects of the RDA cataloging guidelines. Available via the 'Resources' tab of the RDA Toolkit
http://access.rdatoolkit.org/

NLE National Library of Education. One of four national libraries in the U.S., and the library of the U.S. Department of Education. Maintained as part of the Institute of Education Science's National Center for Education Evaluation and Regional Assistance
http://ies.ed.gov/ncee/projects/nle

NLM National Library of Medicine. One of four national libraries in the U.S., and the world's largest biomedical library, covering subjects from medical history to biotechnology
http://www.nlm.nih.gov

NLNZ National Library of New Zealand / Te Puna Mātauranga o Aotearoa. Government-funded cultural and information centre, whose role is to collect and maintain literature and information resources that relate to New Zealand and the Pacific, to make this information readily available, and to preserve New Zealand's documentary heritage for future generations
http://www.natlib.govt.nz

Nobel Prize in Literature A prize, founded by Alfred Bernhard Nobel (1833-1896), awarded annually to the person 'who shall have produced in the field of literature the most distinguished work of an idealistic tendency'
http://www.nobelprize.org/nobel_prizes/literature/

noise 1. Digital transmission: interruption or potential interruption to the transmission of data along analog communication lines. 2. Video: poor quality of picture—grainy, snowy

nom de plume Also pen name, pseudonym. A fictitious name used by an author. Cf allonym, autonym

non-book material Also non-print material. Material other than printed materials—e.g., audiovisual material, computer software

noncirculating Materials available for use within the library, but which may not be borrowed

non-fiction Books based on factual information

non-filing character A character at the start of a MARC field that is not taken into account when filing—e.g., a blank or an initial article

non-print material Also non-book material. Material other than printed materials,—e.g., audiovisual material, computer software

nonresident's card A borrower's card issued, usually for a fee, to a person who does not live in the area served by a library

NOS A contraction of 'not on shelf'. For example, an item in the library that cannot be found on the shelves

Noser Library Research collection of heritage materials, housed within the Friendship Library of the Divine Word University, Papua New Guinea http://www.dwu.ac.pg/en/index.php/the-friendship-library/dwu-libraries#the-noser-library

Notable Books An annual list of significant additions to the world of books, compiled by the Reference and User Services Association of the American Library Association for use by the general reader and librarians who work with adult readers

Notable Children's Books, Recordings, Videos, Websites, Computer Software Annual annotated lists of significant children's resources in the above categories, selected and published by the Association for Library Service to Children, American Library Association

notation The series of symbols that stand for the classes, subclasses, divisions and subdivisions of classes in a classification scheme

note In cataloging, descriptive information that cannot be fitted into other areas of the bibliographic record

not on shelf *See* NOS

novelization, novelisation Converting a work into a novel from another form (e.g., film script, play)

NSLA National and State Libraries Australasia. A group comprising the national libraries of Australia and New Zealand, and the State and Territory libraries of Australia. NSLA members work collaboratively to strengthen the information infrastructure, work on joint projects, and provide a single voice to governments and stakeholders on library and information issues http://www.nsla.org.au/

NT Narrower term. A more specific subject heading. Cf BT, RT

NTIS National Technical Information Service. U.S. Government organization that sells scientific and technical publications published by or associated with the U.S. government
http://www.ntis.gov

NTSC TV/video system used in North and South America, Japan and parts of the Middle East

NUC National Union Catalog. A record of older publications held in libraries in the United States and Canada, many of which do not appear in electronic databases. It is available in print and on microfiche
http://www.loc.gov/rr/main/inforeas/union.html

NUC National Union Catalogue. In Australia, originally a card-based catalog of the holdings of Australian libraries. Now incorporated into Libraries Australia

NUC symbol National Union Catalogue symbol. The Australian library symbol that is a unique identifier for an organization that contributes bibliographic records to the Australian National Bibliographic Database. NUC symbols are used in Libraries Australia Document Delivery (LADD) to indicate a library's holdings for interlibrary loan purposes

number A single issue of a serial in a volume

number building Construction of classification numbers not listed in the schedules, following rules given in the scheme for combining numbers

numeric designation Numbering of a serial in numeric and/or alphabetic form—e.g., Volume 1, number 1. Cf chronological designation

NZGO New Zealand Government Online. A website that provides an overview of New Zealand and its government, access to government services information, and government agency contact details
http://www.govt.nz

NZNB New Zealand National Bibliography. Monthly listing of material published in or about New Zealand and added to *Publications New Zealand*, the online national bibliography. NZNB is available in Word, Excel and PDF formats. Cf Publications New Zealand
http://natlib.govt.nz/librarians/national-library-services/publications-new-zealand

OCLC Online Computer Library Center. A bibliographic network that provides cataloging, resource sharing and reference services worldwide
http://www.oclc.org

OCLC Connexion OCLC's cataloging service—a suite of tools with built-in access to WorldCat, OCLC's database of library bibliographic records
http://www.oclc.org/connexion/

OCLC FirstSearch Also FirstSearch. A collection of reference databases available via the Internet from OCLC
http://www.oclc.org/firstsearch/

octavo 1. A book whose height is between 6 and 9 inches, or 15 and 25 cm. 2. A sheet of paper folded three times to form a section of eight leaves, or sixteen pages. 3. A book having sections of eight leaves, or sixteen pages

Office of Libraries and Archives and Literacy and Awareness Secretariat OLA. Papua New Guinea government department consisting of the National Library Service and the National Archives and Public Records Service

Official Information Act 1982 (OIA) (NZ). New Zealand law to make official information more freely available. It allows people to request and receive information held by any minister, government department or organization including hospitals, schools and state-owned enterprises
http://www.legislation.govt.nz/act/public/1982/0156/latest/DLM64785.html

offprint A copy of an article, chapter, or other portion of a larger work that is reprinted from the same plates but issued separately, usually for the benefit of the author

OH&S Occupational health and safety. Also EH&S, environmental health and safety, WHS, workplace health and safety. Legal requirements for ensuring a safe workplace

OLA Office of Libraries and Archives and Literacy and Awareness Secretariat. Papua New Guinea government department consisting of the National Library Service and the National Archives and Public Records Service

omnibus A volume of reprinted works by one author or on related subjects

on approval New material obtained from a supplier to enable a client to examine it before deciding to buy

on-approval plan Also approval plan. A library's instruction to a publisher or supplier to provide one copy of all publications in a particular category, with the right to return them. Cf blanket order

on-demand publishing *See* demand publishing, print on demand

one person library Also sole charge library. A library managed by one person

ongoing integrating resource A bibliographic resource that is changed by being updated; intended to continue indefinitely—e.g., an organization's website. Cf finite integrating resource

ONIX International standard developed by EDItEUR for representing book industry product information in electronic form
http://www.editeur.org/8/ONIX/

Online Computer Library Center OCLC. A bibliographic network that provides cataloging, resource sharing and reference services worldwide
http://www.oclc.org

online public access catalog, online public access catalogue OPAC. A computer-based catalog that library users access via terminals

online service provider OSP. An organization—e.g., AOL—that provides its own online services in addition to connection to the Internet, or access to a variety of online services, especially databases, usually for a fee

online services The branch of library services that selects and provides access to electronic resources

online workshop Also web conferencing, webinar. Conferences, seminars, workshops and other interactive online conferencing events that can be shared simultaneously across geographically dispersed locations, often via web conferencing services that use cloud computing technologies

on-order file A listing of all items ordered by a library and not yet received

OPAC Online public access catalog, online public access catalogue. A computer-based catalog that library users access via terminals

op. cit. Abbreviation for Latin *opere citato* (in the work cited). Used in a footnote to avoid repeating the full title of a work cited

open access Also open stacks. Where users have direct access to items in the collection. Cf closed access

open entry A bibliographic record that indicates that a serial is still being published (e.g., May 1911-   ). Cf closed entry

open reserve Also reserve collection, restricted loan, short loan. A collection of material in high demand, usually in a teaching institution, whose loan periods are shorter than normal library loans, housed in an area where users have access to the shelves. Cf closed reserve

open source software Software created by a development community rather than a single vendor. The source code is free and available to anyone who wants to use or modify it. Cf public domain software

open stacks Also open access. Where users have direct access to items in the collection. Cf closed access

operating budget Moneys allocated for costs in running a library other than purchasing library material, such as personnel, maintenance, supplies

operating system Software that controls the operation of a computer and its interaction with peripheral equipment—e.g., Windows, Mac OS, LINUX

optical disc A plastic disc that can be read using a light beam, including compact discs, CD-ROMs, laserdiscs and DVDs

oral history 1. Historical information drawn from interviews with participants. 2. The recording or transcript of an interview with a person whose memories are considered worthy of preservation

order number The number on an order when it is placed with a supplier, that identifies all the items on a particular order

orders complete file A listing of orders that have been processed; includes cataloged items and cancelled orders

original cataloging, original cataloguing Cataloging done for the first time, using cataloging tools to create the record

o.s. out of stock. Not presently available from the publisher, but expected

OSP online service provider. An organization—e.g., AOL—that provides its own online services in addition to connection to the Internet, or access to a variety of online services, especially databases, usually for a fee

other title information Also subtitle. Title on a resource other than the title proper or parallel or series title; also any phrase appearing in conjunction with the title proper

out-of-date Not current, old

out-of-print No longer available from the publisher for purchase

out of stock o.s. Not presently available from the publisher, but expected

output 1. The results of processing by a computer system. 2. The signal from a video or audio player

outreach Library programs and services to meet the needs of special categories of users, such as those who are visually-impaired or immobile

outsourcing Contracting to an external organization services that were formerly provided internally

overborrowing Borrowing more items than allowed by the borrowing rules

OverDrive Digital Library Reserve A commercial digital download platform where libraries make e-books, audiobooks, music and videos available for library users to download to their tablets, smartphones or computers http://company.overdrive.com/

overdue Kept beyond the due date

overlay Material that is placed over other material to add to or otherwise alter the information or display

oversize A book that is too large to be shelved in normal sequence on a library's shelves

overuse injury Also repetitive strain injury, repetitive stress injury, RSI. Damage to the hand, wrist or arm, brought about by overuse, often from keyboarding

ownership mark A mark indicating which library owns a particular item. It may be made with a rubber-stamp or embossing machine, or be handwritten

Pacific Islands Association of Libraries, Archives and Museums PIALA. A regional association formed in 1991 to foster awareness and encourage cooperation and resource sharing among libraries, archives and museums and related institutions of the Pacific Islands
http://piala-pacific.wix.com/piala-pacific

Pacific Manuscripts Bureau PAMBU. An archival project established in 1968 and sponsored by major libraries specializing in Pacific research, it makes and distributes microfilm copies of Pacific archives
http://rspas.anu.edu.au/pambu/

Pacific Research Guide A gateway to Internet sites related to the Pacific, maintained by the National Library of Australia
http://www.nla.gov.au/app/eresources/item/4520

page 1. One side of a leaf in a manuscript, book, or other printed publication. 2. Also web page. A screen of a website. 3. A library staff member who delivers materials from closed stacks and reshelves them

pagination 1. The number of pages or leaves (or both) of a book identified in bibliographic description of a book. 2. Dividing a document into pages

PAL TV/video system used in Australia, U.K., South Africa and Western Europe

PAMBU Pacific Manuscripts Bureau. An archival project established in 1968 and sponsored by major libraries specializing in Pacific research, it makes and distributes microfilm copies of Pacific archives
http://rspas.anu.edu.au/pambu/

pamphlet Also booklet. A small (usually less than fifty pages) printed work on a topic of current interest

pamphlet box A box usually made of cardboard, plastic or metal used to store pamphlets and unbound serials

PANDORA Preserving and Accessing Networked Documentary Resources of Australia. A project of the National Library of Australia and other agencies to build an archive of Australian online publications
http://pandora.nla.gov.au/

paper 1. A substance made by breaking down rags, straw, wood, or other fibrous material into pulp, processed into sheets. 2. A document, especially one prepared to be read at a public meeting or conference or published in an academic journal

paperback Also limp, soft cover. Having paper or light card covers. Cf hardback

papermark Also watermark. 1. A faint mark that can be seen in a sheet of good quality paper. 2. A design or lettering printed in grey across a page

papers A collection of personal and family documents, that may include correspondence

Papua New Guinea Library Association PNGLA. Professional association of Papua New Guinean librarians and library officers, established in 1973

Papua New Guinea National Bibliography List of publications received by the National Library of Papua New Guinea on legal deposit

parallel edition Also parallel texts. Different texts of the same work printed on the same page or on facing pages—e.g., a text in its original language and in translation

parallel publishing The simultaneous publication of a work, in print and in electronic format

parallel texts Also parallel edition. Different texts of the same work printed on the same page or on facing pages—e.g., a text in its original language and in translation

parallel title Title proper in another language and/or script

paraphrase To express the same thing in other words

paraprofessional A person trained to assist librarians and able to perform tasks requiring significant knowledge in librarianship, but without a professional (i.e., degree) qualification. Can include library assistants, library officers, library technicians. Cf library technician

PARBICA The Pacific Regional Branch of the International Council on Archives http://www.parbica.org/

parliamentary library A library that provides materials and services to support the work of a national or federal legislature. Cf legislative library

parliamentary paper A document presented to a parliament and ordered by Parliament to be printed. Parliamentary papers include annual reports of government departments and agencies, and reports commissioned by the government for discussion in Parliament

partial title A part of the title that is printed in full on the title page

passim Throughout a work, or very frequently within it

patent An official document conferring the exclusive right or privilege to the proceeds of an invention

pathfinder Also topical guide. Directions to the resources available for a literature search. Cf LibGuides

patron Also client, user. A person who makes use of a service—e.g., a library patron uses the library

patron driven acquisition PDA. Also demand driven acquisition, DDA. An acquisition model usually applied to buying e-books, in which libraries include entries for possible acquisition in their catalog, and a title is triggered for purchase once a significant number of patrons request it

PCC Program for Cooperative Cataloging. An international consortium of institutions working with the Library of Congress, committed to increasing the pool of shareable catalog records created according to agreed standards, including authority records to support all access points http://www.loc.gov/aba/pcc/

PDA patron driven acquisition. Also demand driven acquisition, DDA. An acquisition model usually applied to buying e-books, in which libraries include entries for possible acquisition in their catalog, and a title is triggered for purchase once a significant number of patrons request it

PDF Portable Document Format. A format developed by Adobe for publishing electronic documents, which need Acrobat Reader to access them

peer-reviewed Also refereed. Evaluated by at least one specialist reader, as well as the editor of a scholarly journal, before it is accepted

pen name Also pseudonym, nom de plume. A fictitious name used by an author. Cf allonym, autonym

perfect binding Also adhesive binding. Binding in which the back edge of a volume is trimmed, and adhesive is applied before the case is attached

Performances and Phonograms Treaty *See* WIPO Performances and Phonograms Treaty

periodical A serial with a distinctive title intended to appear in successive parts at stated and regular intervals. Often used as a synonym for serial

periodical index A subject index to a group of periodicals, usually in a general subject area

period order An order from a supplier for items up to a certain total cost, without specifying particular titles

permanent loan An agreement between a library and a user for the user to retain the item 'permanently', unless it is requested by another user

permanent paper Also acid free paper, durable paper. Paper that is pH neutral, and will last longer than paper with acid content

permission Authority to quote passages of text, or to reproduce illustrations, from a published work

persistent identifier A name for a resource on the Web that will remain the same regardless of where the resource is located

persistent uniform resource locator PURL. An Internet address that is used to direct the user to an Internet site via an intermediate resolution service, even if the original URL for the site changes
http://purl.nla.gov.au

personal author Also author. 1. In AACR2, the person chiefly responsible for the intellectual or artistic content of a work. 2. Author: in RDA, a person, family or corporate body responsible for creating a work that is primarily textual in content, regardless of media type (e.g., printed, electronic or tactile text or spoken word) or of genre (e.g., poems, screenplays, blogs). Cf creator

phoenix schedule Completely new development of a section of a classification schedule, where new numbers do not relate to their previous use

phonogram The aural record of sounds of a performance or of other sounds. Cf sound recording

phonogram copyright symbol Also sound recording copyright symbol. The letter 'p' enclosed in a circle ℗, printed on a CD or sound recording to indicate that reproduction of the resource is protected under copyright law

Phonographic Performance Company of Australia PPCA. The organization that grants licenses to broadcast sound recordings in public on behalf of the owners of copyright in sound recordings
http://www.ppca.com.au

phonograph record Also gramophone record, vinyl record. A sound disc made of vinyl plastic, with sound grooves pressed into the surface

photographic material Material composed of at least two layers: the image carrier (usually gelatine) and the support (usually paper or polyester)

physical carrier The physical medium in which data, sound, images etc. are stored — e.g., the compact disc on which music is recorded. Cf container, carrier/carrier type

physical description In AACR2, information about the physical form of an item — e.g., pagination, type of recording, dimensions. RDA cataloging uses the terms 'extent', 'content', 'dimensions' and 'carrier type' for this concept

physical processing Also end processing, process, processing. To prepare an item for use in the library or for loan. This can include affixing library stamps, barcodes, call number labels, dust covers, etc.

PIALA Pacific Islands Association of Libraries, Archives and Museums. A regional association formed in 1991 to foster awareness and encourage cooperation and resource sharing among libraries, archives and museums and related institutions of the Pacific Islands
http://piala-pacific.wix.com/piala-pacific

Picture Australia An Internet-based service that enabled users to search many significant Australian online pictorial collections at the same time. Now integrated into Trove

picture book A book of pictures with little or no text, usually intended for children

picture file A collection of illustrations, art prints, photographs, and clippings usually stored in a filing cabinet

picture library A library that collects mainly visual documents (photographs, engravings, prints, etc.)

pinyin System of romanization of Chinese characters, generally recognized as the standard throughout the world

plate A full page of illustration on a leaf that is usually on paper of a different quality than the text

playaway 1. An mp3 player that contains one pre-loaded audiobook. 2. The trade name of the company that developed the original playaway device

PLR Public lending right. A payment made to authors by government in respect of their works lent by public libraries

PMC PubMed Central. A free full-text archive of biomedical and life sciences journal articles at the U.S. National Library of Medicine
http://www.ncbi.nlm.nih.gov/pmc/

PMC Canada PubMed Central Canada. A free online full-text archive of published, peer-reviewed Canadian health and life sciences research
http://pubmedcentralcanada.ca/pmcc/

PNGLA Papua New Guinea Library Association. Professional association of Papua New Guinean librarians and library officers, established in 1973

PNG National Bibliography List of publications received by the National Library of Papua New Guinea on legal deposit

pocket edition A book small enough to be carried in a coat pocket

POD Also print on demand, publishing on demand, electronic publishing on demand, EPOD. A type of publishing using digital printing technology, in which a book or other publication is printed on an as-needed basis, allowing small print runs and dispensing with the need for warehousing stock

point of service Also service point. An area in a library where staff provide specific services—e.g., circulation desk, reference desk

point-of-use instruction Advice on how to use a research tool or resource (e.g., database, index, etc.) at the time when the user needs help

policy paper *See* white paper

polyglot dictionary A dictionary that provides translations of each word into more than one other language

Popular Paperbacks for Young Adults Annual annotated lists of recommended paperbacks from popular genres or topics of current interest to teens, selected by the Young Adult Library Services Association, American Library Association

pop-up book A novelty children's book whose illustrations become three dimensional when a page is opened

pornography Sexually explicit material that lacks artistic value. Cf erotica

portal Also gateway, subject gateway. An entry point to the Internet that provides access to electronic information including websites, ftp sites, databases and indexes to print resources in a subject area such as agriculture

post 1. To send a message to a mailing list or newsgroup. 2. To publish information on the Internet

post binding A form of loose-leaf binding in which rigid posts are inserted through pre-punched holes in the leaves, allowing leaves to be added or removed individually. Cf ring binding

post-coordinate 1. Of subject headings or other search terms, put together by the user at the time of searching. 2. Refers to terms used for searching an online index or database, where the computer combines the terms to carry out the search. Cf pre-coordinate

posthumous Published for the first time after the death of the author

PPCA Phonographic Performance Company of Australia. The organization that grants licenses to broadcast sound recordings in public on behalf of the owners of the copyright
http://www.ppca.com.au

practicum Also work experience (Australian usage). A period of work in an information agency to gain practical experience

preamble An introductory statement to a document, describing its purpose

precataloging, precataloguing Bibliographic searching, usually done before ordering an item, to establish correct bibliographic information

precedence order The order in which instructions are to be followed

precis A summary that captures the basic idea expressed in a larger work

precision A measure of the accuracy of database searching

pre-coordinate Of subject headings or other search terms, put together by the cataloger or indexer. Cf post-coordinate

preface The author's or editor's reasons for the book. It appears after the title page and before the introduction

preferred name In RDA cataloging, the form of name chosen to identify a person, family or corporate body. It is the basis for the authorized access point representing that entity

preferred sources of information In RDA cataloging, the places where information that can be used to create a bibliographic description are found. These include the resources themselves and in some cases reference tools or catalogs about the resources. Cf chief source of information

preferred title for the work In RDA cataloging, the title chosen to identify a resource at the work level. This is used as the basis for the authorized access point representing that work

preliminary pages The material at the beginning of a book including contents, introduction, foreword

prepayment Payment made with a purchase order, before goods are sent

preprint A portion of a work that is made available before the whole is published—e.g., an article in a periodical or a piece from an anthology

prescriptive dictionary Defines words in a dictionary and lays down standards of acceptability and usage. Cf descriptive dictionary

presentation copy A copy of a book that is inscribed by the author, illustrator, or editor

preservation Changing the state of library material in order to protect the content—e.g., microfilming newspapers. Cf conservation

presidential library A special library whose collection consists of the papers of a former president of the United States and other relevant documents

press clipping service Also media monitoring. A service that examines the press, radio and television regularly for information on specific topics, and reports to requesting clients

primary access point Access point used as the initial element in citing a work

primary source A document that provides first-hand knowledge of an event, including personal papers, photographs, etc. Cf secondary source

Prime Minister's Literary Awards Australian federal government awards rewarding excellence in Australian literature and history, and celebrating the contribution these make to the nation's cultural and intellectual life http://arts.gov.au/funding-support/awards/prime-ministers-literary-awards

Primo Discovery layer software from Ex Libris. Cf discovery layer

print on demand Also POD, publishing on demand, electronic publishing on demand, EPOD. A type of publishing using digital printing technology, in which a book or other publication is printed on an as-needed basis, allowing small print runs and dispensing with the need for warehousing stock

privately published Published at the author's expense. Cf vanity press

problem patron A user who disturbs the functioning of the library

proceedings The published record of a meeting or conference sponsored by an academic society or other organization

process, processing Also end processing, physical processing. To prepare an item for use in the library or for loan. This can include affixing library stamps, barcodes, call number labels, dust covers, etc.

Procite Computer software for handling bibliographic data and converting it into bibliographies, owned by Thomson Reuters. Sales and support discontinued in 2013, except for support in converting to another Reuters product, EndNote. Cf EndNote

production statement In RDA, a statement identifying the place of production, the producer, and date of production of an unpublished resource

professional Having a university or equivalent qualification in librarianship or information management, and performing work at a professional level

professional development Activity that increases a person's professional knowledge and/or skills. Cf continuing professional development

professional ethics A statement of the ethical principles that guide professional workers in carrying out their work. Many library associations have formal codes of ethics for their members

profile 1. An outline of the interest area(s) of a user or a group of users, used by the library to identify new information of interest to particular users. 2. An indication to a library supplier of the subject areas in which materials should/should not be supplied

program-based budgeting Financial planning that considers all the activities or programs in an area and bids for funds to run these programs

Program for Cooperative Cataloging PCC. An international consortium of institutions working with the Library of Congress, committed to increasing the pool of shareable catalog records created according to mutually agreed standards, including authority records to support all access points
http://www.loc.gov/aba/pcc/

Project Gutenberg A volunteer effort to digitize and archive cultural works in the public domain. It is one of the earliest digital libraries and offers free e-books to users. Founded in the U.S., there are many affiliated organizations worldwide
http://www.gutenberg.org/

projection A particular way of representing the earth (three-dimensional) on a map (two-dimensional)

prologue An introduction to a play or other work, usually included in the text. Cf epilogue

proofing, proofreading Checking a printer's proof for errors

ProQuest An online service that provides access to indexes, abstracts, full-text and image databases in a range of subject areas
http://www.proquest.com

ProQuest Dialog Formerly Dialog Corporation. Online information company providing online-based information services in business, science, engineering, pharmaceuticals, finance and patents. Founded in 1972, now part of ProQuest
http://www.dialog.com/

ProQuest Dissertations & Theses A commercial database providing access to full-text, long abstracts, and citations of dissertations worldwide, with an emphasis on U.S. and Canadian dissertations
http://www.proquest.com/products-services/pqdt.html

protocol 1. A set of guidelines, regulations and requirements agreed to by all parties, often international agreements—e.g. the ISO interlibrary loan protocol. 2. An agreed set of rules by which messages passed from one computer system to another are encoded and interpreted

provenance 1. The origin or source. 2. A record of previous ownership of a work. 3. The archival principle of not mingling records of different creators

provincial library A public library serving a province across local and community boundaries

proximity operator Also adjacency operator. A word or symbol that enables searching of terms close to each other in a title etc.—e.g., near, with

pseudonym Also pen name, nom de plume. A fictitious name used by an author. Cf allonym, autonym

publication The issuing of copies of a book or other item to the public

Publications New Zealand New Zealand's national bibliography, available online. It covers material published in New Zealand or with a significant NZ content, and links to libraries for finding each item. A metadata dataset and monthly reports of new records added are available. Cf NZNB
http://natlib.govt.nz/librarians/national-library-services/publications-new-zealand

publication statement In RDA, a statement identifying the place of publication, the publisher, and date of publication of a resource

public domain Not (or no longer) protected by copyright

public domain software Programs available for public use free of charge. Cf open source software

public lending right PLR. A payment made to authors by government in respect of their works lent by public libraries

public library A library funded by government that provides library services to all sections of the community

public relations Outreach and community activities that promote the library

public services Also client services, reader services. Direct services to library users, including circulation, interlibrary loan, bibliographic instruction, and reference services. Cf reference services

publish 1. To issue in printed form—e.g., a book, serial. 2. To issue in non-book form —e.g., a videorecording, computer software. 3. To make available via the Internet

published price Also list price. The publisher's advertised, undiscounted price

publisher A person or body issuing copies of a book or other item to the public

publishing on demand Also POD, print on demand, electronic publishing on demand, EPOD. A type of publishing using digital printing technology, in which a book or other publication is printed on an as-needed basis, allowing small print runs and dispensing with the need for warehousing stock.

PubMed A searchable database that includes MEDLINE citations as well as citations to online books, other biomedical literature and some links to full-text content from PubMed Central and publisher websites. Cf MEDLINE
http://www.nlm.nih.gov/bsd/pmresources.html

PubMed Central PMC. A free full-text archive of biomedical and life sciences journal articles at the U.S. National Library of Medicine
http://www.ncbi.nlm.nih.gov/pmc/

PubMed Central Canada PMC Canada. A free online full-text archive of published, peer-reviewed Canadian health and life sciences research
http://pubmedcentralcanada.ca/pmcc/

puff (American usage) Also blurb. Description of a book by the publisher, usually found on the back cover or book jacket, or in an advertising brochure or catalog

Pulitzer Prizes Annual prizes for fiction, biography or autobiography, drama, poetry, history of the United States and non-fiction, established in 1917 as willed by Joseph Pulitzer
http://www.pulitzer.org/

pull technology Technology in which a user specifically asks for something by performing a search or requesting an existing file—e.g., when browsing the Web. Cf push technology

pulp fiction Sensational fictional work of no literary value

purchase order An order placed with a supplier, usually by a government department or agency, that indicates a firm intention to purchase

pure notation One type of symbol only—e.g., numbers—used as the notation of a classification scheme. Cf mixed notation

PURL Persistent uniform resource locator. An Internet address that is used to direct the user to an Internet site via an intermediate resolution service, even if the original URL for the site changes
http://purl.nla.gov.au

push technology Technology in which selected data is automatically delivered to a user's computer at prescribed intervals or based on a specific event—e.g., RSS feeds. Cf pull technology

put room Place to put returned materials before shelving them

PVC Poly vinyl chloride. Not recommended for storage of library materials as it deteriorates, giving off vapours that tarnish the material

qualifier An addition to a name etc., enclosed in parentheses

quarterly (adj) Issued four times a year. (n) A publication issued four times a year

quarto 1. A book over 25 and under 30 cm high. 2. A sheet of paper folded twice to form a section of four leaves. 3. A book having sections of four leaves, or eight pages

query A question, especially a search request put to a database

QuestionPoint Formerly Collaborative Digital Reference Service. A web-based virtual reference service and set of administrative tools for libraries, developed by the Library of Congress and OCLC and advised by the Global Reference Network
http://www.questionpointorg/

Quick Picks for Reluctant Young Adult Readers An annual annotated list of recommended books appropriate for reluctant young readers, selected by the Young Adult Library Services Association, American Library Association

q.v. Abbreviation for Latin *quod vide* (which see). Used in reference works to refer the user to another term in the same work

RAD Rules for Archival Description. A set of rules for describing archival material, developed by Canadian archivists and based on the *Anglo-American Cataloguing Rules (AACR)*

radio frequency identification RFID. Technology in which clients pass their library card over a self-checking unit to register their borrower details

range A set of shelving bays

rare book A book of which very few copies still exist

RCIP/CHIN Réseau canadien d'information sur le patrimoine / Canadian Heritage Information Network. A network of Canadian museums and heritage organizations that aims to promote the development, presentation and preservation of Canada's digital heritage
http://www.chin.gc.ca/

RDA *Resource Description and Access*. Descriptive cataloging rules replacing the *Anglo-American Cataloguing Rules (AACR2)*, intended for use by libraries and other cultural collecting organizations. Released in 2010 and implemented by major collections beginning in 2013
http://www.rdatoolkit.org/

RDC Research Data Canada. A multi-discipline organization of universities, institutes, libraries and researchers who develop and promote strategy on the access and preservation of data arising from Canadian research
http://rds-sdr.cisti-icist.nrc-cnrc.gc.ca/eng/

reader education, reader instruction Also bibliographic instruction, client education, library orientation, user education. Helping people to derive the most benefit from using the library

readers' advisor A library staff member who advises readers on their choice of books and generally assists in the use of the resources of the library

readers' advisor's desk Also enquiry desk, help desk, information desk, reference desk. The area of a library where staff help people to use the library and answer requests for information

reader services Also client services, public services. Direct services to library users, including circulation, interlibrary loan, bibliographic instruction, and reference services. Cf reference services

reading group A group formed to discuss books the members have read

reading room A room in a library that is used mainly for reading and study

ready reference Standard reference books kept close to the reference desk to enable reference librarians to locate factual information

ready reference query A question requiring factual information from one simple source

realia Three-dimensional objects

real-time online reference service A reference service in which librarians respond to online user enquiries immediately

real-time processing Also transaction processing. Processing that updates information immediately. Cf batch processing

reasonable portion An allowable amount to copy, according to copyright legislation—e.g., in Australia 10% of the total number of pages, or one chapter, of a published work that is of not less than 10 pages and is not an artistic work, or one or more periodical articles on the same subject. The copyright acts of various countries may contain different definitions of reasonable portions for different formats of material

rebinding The complete reconstruction of a book, usually by resewing pages and applying a new cover

recall (n) 1. A request for the return from loan of a library item. 2. Retrieval of information from a database. (v) To request the return of a library loan

recataloging, recataloguing Revising catalog records because of a change in library policy or needs

receiver A unit of audio or audio/video equipment that acts as the control panel for a stereo or home theatre system

reciprocal borrowing The exchange of borrowing privileges between two libraries

reclassification 1. Revision of call numbers. 2. Converting a collection from one classification scheme to another

Recommended Retail Price RRP. The price at which the publisher recommends that booksellers sell the item

record (n) 1. A document. 2. The data relating to a document—e.g., in a catalog or database. (v) 1. To preserve information in writing, typescript or coded form. 2. To reproduce sound and/or pictures using disc or magnetic tape. 3. In RDA cataloging, to use the information found on a resource, or in another source, to create a bibliographic record. One can adjust the information slightly if required for readability or presentation purposes. Cf transcribe

Records and Information Management Professionals Australasia RIM Professionals Australasia. The peak professional association for the records and information management industry in Oceania http://www.rimpa.com.au/

records management The control of the administrative records of an organization

record status Byte 5 of the MARC leader. The most common values are **n** for new record and **c** for changed record

record structure The organization of the MARC record into the leader, the directory and the variable fields

recto The right-hand page of an open book. Cf verso

reduction Making a classification number shorter by omitting one or more groups of digits from the end of the number

refereed Also peer-reviewed. Evaluated by at least one specialist reader, as well as the editor of a scholarly journal, before it is accepted

reference A direction from one heading or entry to another. Cf see reference, see also reference

reference book Also reference work. A resource intended to be consulted for factual information on specific matters, rather than read

reference collection A collection of books intended to be consulted for specific facts, rather than read. Usually not for loan outside the library

reference desk Also enquiry desk, help desk, information desk, readers' adviser's desk. The area of a library where staff help people to use the library and answer requests for information

reference interview The face-to-face exchange between a librarian and a reader to communicate, refine or clarify a reference enquiry

reference librarian A librarian working at the information or reference desk, or otherwise delivering service to users

reference question A request by a library user for information or help finding it

reference services Services to library users including reader education, meeting users' requests for specific information and assistance, and managing the use of library material and equipment. Cf client services, reader services, public services

reference source A source of authoritative information relied upon by a reference librarian to answer a query

reference stacks The shelves where reference books are housed

reference strategy The process of finding answers to reference queries in the fastest, most efficient way

reference work 1. Also reference book. A resource intended to be consulted for factual information on specific matters, rather than read. 2. The work of the library that provides assistance to users seeking information

regional library A public library serving a district, usually across local government boundaries

registration Joining the library

reissue A second or subsequent impression of an edition in which the cover and/or title page are redesigned but the text remains substantially the same

related term RT. A subject heading at the same level of specificity to another heading and related in subject matter. Cf broader term, narrower term

relational operator A word or symbol that enables a searcher to specify greater than, less than etc.—e.g., >= 1992 means published in or after 1992

relationship In RDA cataloging, the link between and among entities, often recorded using access points controlled by authority records. Relationships give users pathways to other relevant material

relationship designator In RDA, a term that indicates the nature of the relationship to or between entities. Relationship designators are listed in vocabularies that enable catalogers to describe relationships consistently

relative index In a classification scheme, an alphabetical list of all topics and synonyms, showing the relation of the topics to all the disciplines they are associated with

relative location Items are placed in relationship to others depending on the subject

relevance, relevancy The degree to which retrieved items match the requirements of a search

relief map Also contour map. A map that shows elevations on the surface of the earth and beneath the oceans by means of contour lines, shading, etc.

relocated topic A subject that has been allocated a different number in a classification scheme

remainder list 1. A list issued by a publisher or bookseller of material to be sold at or below cost price. 2. A list of unwanted or duplicate items circulated to other libraries to request before they are disposed of

renew 1. To extend the period for which a library item is on loan. 2. To extend the length of a serial subscription

rental collection A collection whose items are lent for a fee

repeatable Able to be used more than once within a record—e.g., some MARC fields and subfields are repeatable in a bibliographic record

repetitive strain injury, repetitive stress injury RSI. Also overuse injury. Damage to the hand, wrist or arm, brought about by overuse, often from keyboarding

replacement A resource purchased by a library to take the place of a lost or worn-out copy of the same title

replica A copy or reproduction of a resource, especially one made by the creator of the original

report 1. A record of research findings. 2. An official record of the activities of a corporate entity. 3. A formal account of an investigation

repository A place where material, for example archival material, is stored. Cf institutional repository

reprint A new printing of a work made from the original type face

reprographic reproduction Copying an item, especially by photocopying

republication Reissuing a published resource by a different publisher, without altering the text

Request for Information RFI. A request to system vendors/developers, giving an overview of requirements for a system and asking how they could be met

Request for Proposals RFP. A formal request to system vendors/developers to submit proposals for system development

Request for Tender RFT. A formal request to supply products or services, usually in response to a defined set of specifications or criteria

requisition A formal request for the purchase of materials, supplies or services

research collection 1. Library material that can sustain research in a particular subject. 2. Holdings of a research library

Research Data Canada RDC. A multi-discipline organization of universities, institutes, libraries and researchers who develop and promote strategy on the access and preservation of data arising from Canadian research
http://rds-sdr.cisti-icist.nrc-cnrc.gc.ca/eng/

research guide Advice on strategies and resources for investigating a topic

research library A library committed to supporting long-term scholarly activity

research query A question requiring complex information that cannot be obtained from a single source

Réseau canadien d'information sur le patrimoine / Canadian Heritage Information Network RCIP/CHIN. A network of Canadian museums and heritage organizations that aims to promote the development, presentation and preservation of Canada's digital heritage
http://www.chin.gc.ca/

reserve To request an item as soon as it is returned from loan or otherwise made ready for borrowing

reserve collection Also closed reserve, open reserve, restricted loan, short loan. A collection of material in high demand, usually in a teaching institution, whose access is controlled and whose loan periods are shorter than normal library loans

reshelve To replace items on the shelf in order

reshelving cart Also book truck. A wheeled trolley used for returning books to their shelves or other areas in the library

resource A term used in RDA for any Group I entity (work, expression, manifestation or item) or group or components of such entities, either tangible (e.g., an audiocassette, three sheet maps) or intangible (e.g., a website)

resource center, resource centre A library in a school or other educational institution or network. Cf learning hub

Resource Description and Access RDA. Descriptive cataloging rules replacing the *Anglo-American Cataloguing Rules (AACR2)*, intended for use by libraries and other cultural collecting organizations. Released in 2010 and implemented by major collections beginning in 2013 http://www.rdatoolkit.org/

resource discovery Location of documents, especially on the World Wide Web

resource sharing The sharing of material between libraries, such as where an expensive item is purchased by one library and made available to others

response time Also access time. The time an online system takes to respond to a user's command. Cf turnaround time

restricted access Can only be seen or used by certain people

restricted loan Also closed reserve, open reserve, reserve collection, short loan. A collection of material in high demand, usually in a teaching institution, whose access is controlled and whose loan periods are shorter than normal library loans

restricted publication A publication restricted to a particular category of reader—e.g., over 18s (for some overtly sexual material), Defence Force personnel (for classified material)

retrospective bibliography A bibliography of materials published in a specified past period. Cf current bibliography

retrospective conversion Changing older records, usually from a printed card catalog into machine-readable form

Reuters A major international news agency providing online news and information services; the news and media division of Thomson Reuters http://www.reuters.com

review article An article that analyses all aspects of a topic or issue

review publication A journal that mainly publishes reviews of new books and other material—e.g. *New York review of books*

revised edition, revision A new edition of a work containing alterations and/or additions. Cf continuous revision, named revision

RFI Request for Information. A request to system vendors/developers, giving an overview of requirements for a system and asking how they could be met

RFID Radio frequency identification. Technology in which clients pass their library card over a self-checking unit to register their borrower details

RFP Request for Proposals. A formal request to system vendors/developers to submit proposals for system development

RFT Request for Tender. A formal request to supply products or services, usually in response to a defined set of specifications or criteria

rhetoric 1. The art or branch of knowledge that treats the rules or principles underlying all effective composition, whether in prose or verse. 2. The art that teaches oratory

rhyming dictionary A dictionary for writers of poetry, listing words of a language alphabetically by phonetic ending

right truncation Abbreviation of a search term using a special symbol, such as #, *, used at the end of the search term

RIM Professionals Australasia Records and Information Management Professionals Australasia. The peak professional association for the records and information management industry in Oceania http://www.rimpa.com.au/

ring binding Loose-leaf binding in which pages with punched holes are placed on metal rings attached to the spine of the binder, allowing them to be added or removed. Cf post binding

romanization, romanisation Rendering of the letters or characters of another alphabet into those of the Latin alphabet

Roman numeral A number like I, II, III, IV, ... or i, ii, iii, iv ...

Round Table A membership unit of the American Library Association established to promote a field of librarianship not within the scope of any single division

routing 1. Circulating an item, especially an issue of a serial, to a specified list of users, each of whom sends it to the next person when they have finished with it. 2. Finding a path through a network to a computer, usually handled by the communications hardware and software

routing slip A list of users to whom an item, especially an issue of a serial, is to be circulated

roving librarian A reference librarian who works from the floor of the library, aiding those who ask for help and/or identifying patrons who appear to need help and actively approaching them to offer assistance

roving reference An approach to reference services that advocates moving reference activities to the floor of the library, rather than passively waiting behind a reference desk for users to approach with queries

royalty Payment to an author by a publisher, based on a percentage of the price of the book, and paid for every book sold

rpm Revolutions per minute. Measurement of the speed of play of a phonograph record

RRP Recommended retail price. The price at which the publisher recommends that booksellers sell the item

RSI repetitive strain injury, repetitive stress injury. Also overuse injury. Damage to the hand, wrist or arm brought about by overuse, often from keyboarding

RSS, RSS feed A 'push' technology in which online publishers send changes of frequently updated website content directly to users, eliminating the need for the user to check the website regularly

RT Related term. A subject heading at the same level of specificity to another heading and related in subject matter. Cf BT, NT

Rules for Archival Description RAD. A set of rules for describing archival material, developed by Canadian archivists and based on the *Anglo-American Cataloguing Rules (AACR)*

running head The book or chapter title at the top of each page. In a periodical the running head may give full bibliographic information

running number A number added in the order in which the item has been received or processed

running title A title or shortened title that appears at the top or bottom of the pages of a work, usually a serial

rural library A library that serves people in the countryside and in villages

SACO Subject Authority Cooperative Program. The subject authority component of the Library of Congress' Program for Cooperative Cataloging http://www.loc.gov/aba/pcc/saco/index.html

sacred work A basic writing of a religion, such as *The Bible, Koran, Talmud* etc., that is generally accepted by followers of the religion

Safari A web browser for Apple Mac computers
http://www.apple.com/safari/

sample stocktaking Checking a sample of the collection against the record of the library's holdings—e.g., checking every 100th book. Cf complete stocktaking, continuous stocktaking

SAN Standard Address Number. A unique identification number assigned to an organization in or served by the book trade, particularly those involved in electronic transfer of information
https://www.myidentifiers.com.au/san/main

SBC/BSC La Société bibliographique du Canada / Bibliographical Society of Canada. A society that promotes bibliographical activity and research
http://www.bsc-sbc.ca/

scale The ratio of distances on a map to the corresponding values on the earth

scan 1. To examine every item in a collection to determine usefulness for information retrieval. 2. To read a printed document into a computer

scatter indexing Indexing a term under two or more headings

schedule The enumerated classes, divisions etc. of a classification scheme, arranged in number order. Cf table

Scholarly Publishing and Academic Resources Coalition SPARC. An alliance of universities, research libraries, and organizations focused on expanding the dissemination of research information
http://www.sparc.arl.org/

scholars' centre A dedicated area of a university library focused on the needs of postgraduate students and academic staff

school librarian Also teacher-librarian. A librarian who manages a school library and offers a library service to students and staff of a school

school library A library in a school that offers a library service to students and staff

School Library Bill of Rights A policy statement by the Australian School Library Association that school libraries should provide materials that enrich the curriculum and stimulate critical thinking in order to develop informed and responsible citizens. Cf Library Bill of Rights

Schools Cataloguing Information Service SCIS. An Australian national cataloging network for schools, maintained through the cooperation of the state and territory education departments
http://www2.curriculum.edu.au/scis/home.html

SCI/ISC Société canadienne d'indexation / Indexing Society of Canada. Canada's national association of professional indexers
http://indexers.ca/

SCIS Schools Cataloguing Information Service. An Australian national cataloging network for schools, maintained through the cooperation of the state and territory education departments
http://www2.curriculum.edu.au/scis/home.html

scope The range of subjects covered by an index, abstracting service, database, reference book, etc.

scope note A note describing the range and meaning of a subject term or classification number

score A printed or written version of a musical work in musical notation

Screenrights The Australian copyright collecting society for rightsholders in film, radio and television
http://www.screen.org

scroll (n) A roll of parchment or other material on which text can be written. (v) To cause text or images to move horizontally or vertically across a computer screen

SDI selective dissemination of information. A service where users are notified regularly of new information according to a profile of interest areas. Cf CAS

seamless searching Searching in which users are unaware that different sources of information are being accessed, since they can use the same commands, procedures etc. and the interface does not change. Cf federated search, discovery layer

SEAPAVAA Southeast Asia–Pacific Audiovisual Archives Association. An association that provides a regional forum for addressing common issues and concerns related to the collection and preservation of, and provision of access to, the audiovisual heritage of member countries
http://archives.pia.gov.ph/seapavaa/

search engine Software that locates information in a database or set of databases, especially on the Internet

search history A sequential list of searches conducted during a session

search service An agency that finds out-of-print or rare materials

search software A computer program that causes a search for information to be carried out in an online catalog or electronic database

search statement An information query entered in a form that a specific searching system can understand

search strategy 1. The approach adopted to finding information on a particular topic. 2. The search statements used to answer an enquiry

search syntax Also syntax. The order of entering computer search terms, that governs the order in which the operations are carried out

search term A word, phrase or number entered by a user to find the records in a database that match the term

Sears List of Subject Headings An authoritative list of subject headings used widely in school and public libraries. Available in print and online

SECAM TV/video system used in France, Russia and parts of the Middle East

secondary source A work that reports or interprets an event using first-hand documents. Cf primary source

Second List of Australian Subject Headings SLASH. A list of specifically Australian headings compiled to supplement Library of Congress Subject Headings. Cf Australian Subject Access Project https://www.nla.gov.au/librariesaustralia/about/expert-advisory-groups/subject-headings-review-panel/australian-subject-access-project/

second summary of Dewey Decimal Classification The 100 divisions, each of which represents a broad topic

section 1. A component of a serial, or of a law book, published separately. 2. A distinct portion of a book, newspaper, or journal. 3. A unit of library shelving

security system An electronic alarm system at the exit of a library building to prevent the theft of materials

see also reference A direction from one heading to another when both are used. In cataloging, RDA uses the term 'authorized access point'

see reference A direction from one heading, which is not used, to another heading that is used. In cataloging, RDA uses the term 'variant access point'

segmentation The division of classification numbers into meaningful parts, with a view to abbreviating them for a particular library

segregated shelving The different formats of library materials are shelved separately according to their needs. Cf integrated shelving

Selected Videos for Young Adults An annual annotated list of videos especially significant to young adults, selected by the Young Adult Library Services Association, American Library Association

selection The process of choosing which items to add to a library's collection

selection aid A tool used to choose new library material—e.g., a book review journal

selection criteria The basis on which the library decides which items to add to its collection

selection policy The policy according to which the library decides what to add to the collection

selective dissemination of information SDI. A service where users are notified regularly of new information according to a profile of interest areas. Cf current awareness service

self-checkout A facility for library users to register their own loans

semiannual Also half yearly. Issued every six months

semimonthly Issued twice a month

semiweekly Issued twice a week

sentencing In records management, deciding where and for how long records should be kept

separately paginated Numbering the pages of each volume or part, or each issue of a periodical, in a separate series, starting with number one. Cf continuous pagination

serial A resource issued in successive parts, usually bearing numbering, that has no predetermined conclusion. One of RDA's four modes of issuance. Includes reproductions of serials, and also resources that exhibit characteristics of serials but whose duration is limited—e.g., newsletters of events. Cf monograph

serial issue A single copy of a serial title

seriality The concept of continuity, of successive instalments of a publication

serial record The bibliographic and purchase details of a serial—title, publisher, holdings, supplier, cost, etc.

serial record card The financial record of a serial—supplier, cost, etc.—in a manual serials system

Serials Directory Trade bibliography for serials published by EBSCO. Lists all current serials published anywhere in the world
http://www.ebscohost.com/public/the-serials-directory

Serials in Australian Libraries SIAL. A bibliographic database listing the locations of over 663,000 serials held in Australian libraries. Available online from Informit http://www.informit.com.au/indexes_SIAL.html

serial title The title of all issues of a serial. Some serials also give titles to individual issues

series A group of separate resources related to each other by the fact that they have a collective title applying to the group as a whole, as well as each resource having its own title proper. Individual resources in a series may or may not be numbered. Cf monographic series

series title The collective title of a group of monographs or other resources, each of which also has an individual title

series title page In monographic series, an added title page in each monograph bearing the series title and sometimes a list of all the works in the series

service point Also point of service. An area in a library where staff provide specific services—e.g., circulation desk, reference desk

shared cataloging, shared cataloguing Also cooperative cataloging. Sharing of catalog records by participating libraries

shared responsibility Also single statement of responsibility. Collaboration between two or more persons or bodies performing the same function in the creation of a work. Cf mixed responsibility

shareware Software sold for a small fee. Users may try it out before deciding to buy. Cf freeware

shelf dummy A piece of solid material with a label that indicates where a particular item, shelved out of the normal sequence, is located, such as a volume of a periodical on microfilm

shelf guide A sign to show the sequence of call numbers in a set of shelves

shelf list A record of the books and other resources in a library in the order in which they are shelved

shelf read To check the order of the materials on the shelves

shelve To place material in order on the shelves

short loan Also closed reserve, open reserve, reserve collection, restricted loan. A collection of material in high demand, usually in a teaching institution, whose access is controlled and whose loan periods are shorter than normal library loans

shutter A device in a projector or camera, made of a thin metal disc with two or three blades, that blocks the passage of light through the aperture while the film is moved or a photograph is taken

SIAL Serials in Australian Libraries. A bibliographic database listing the locations of over 663,000 serials held in Australian libraries. Available online from Informit
http://www.informit.com.au/indexes_SIAL.html

signature 1. The identifying details of a writer at the end of an email message. 2. Section of a book, usually 8, 16 or 32 pages, stitched together

signature binding Form of binding where the signatures are stitched together and encased in boards

silverfish Small insect that eats the protein and starch components of paper and the adhesives in book bindings, causing damage to book, photo and textile collections. Cf bookworm

simultaneous publication Publishing the same book at the same time in different countries or regions. Cf co-publishing

Singapore/Malaysia Collection SMC. Databases from the National University of Singapore Library, with references to Singapore, Malaysia, Brunei and ASEAN. Contain records from 1900 to 2007. No longer updated. Available online as an archived database from Informit
http://www.informit.com.au/indexes_SMC.html

single statement of responsibility Also shared responsibility. Collaboration between two or more persons or bodies performing the same function in the creation of a work. Cf multiple statements of responsibility, statement of responsibility

s.l. Abbreviation of Latin *sine loco* (without place). Place of publication not known. Used in AACR2 cataloging. RDA cataloging uses the term 'Place of publication not identified'

SLA Special Libraries Association. An organization founded in 1909, with an international membership of information professionals who work in special libraries serving business, research, government, etc.
http://www.sla.org/

SLASH Second List of Australian Subject Headings. A list of specifically Australian headings compiled to supplement Library of Congress Subject Headings. Cf Australian Subject Access Project
https://www.nla.gov.au/librariesaustralia/about/expert-advisory-groups/subject-headings-review-panel/australian-subject-access-project/

sleeve A transparent plastic cover that fits a hardcover book and protects it against wear

slide projector A piece of equipment used for showing small photographic transparencies

slipcase A protective box with one open end, for storing books or other items

smart card A small plastic card with a built-in microprocessor and memory

SMC Singapore/Malaysia Collection. Databases from the National University of Singapore Library, with references to Singapore, Malaysia, Brunei and ASEAN. Contains records from 1900 to 2007. No longer updated. Available online as an archived database from Informit
http://www.informit.com.au/indexes_SMC.html

s.n. Abbreviation of Latin *sine nomine* (without name). Name of publisher not known. Used in AACR2 cataloging. RDA cataloging uses the term 'Publisher not identified'

Société bibliographique du Canada / Bibliographical Society of Canada SBC/BSC. A society that promotes bibliographical activity and research
http://www.bsc-sbc.ca/

Société canadienne d'indexation / Indexing Society of Canada SCI/ISC. Canada's national association of professional indexers
http://indexers.ca/

Société Internationale des Bibliothèques et des Musées des Arts du Spectacle / International Association of Libraries and Museums of the Performing Arts An organization concerned with the documentation of the performing arts, including the development of reference works and cataloging standards
http://www.sibmas.org/

soft cover Also limp, paperback. Having paper or light card covers. Cf hardback

software 1. Audiovisual material—e.g., slides, 16mm motion picture etc. 2. Computer program(s), that tells the computer what to do. Cf hardware

sole charge library Also one person library. A library managed by one person

Solomon Islands National Library Service The library service of the Solomon Islands, including the national library and the public library service
http://www.solomonencyclopaedia.net/biogs/E000212b.htm

sorting 1. Display of results of a search in a specified order, such as by date of publication. 2. Placing library materials in call number order prior to shelving

Sound Archives / Ngā Taonga Kōrero New Zealand's foremost radio archive, responsible for managing, collecting, preserving and providing access to the nation's recorded radio heritage
http://www.soundarchives.co.nz/

sound recording Any format of recorded sound, including audiotape, compact disc, phonograph record

sound recording copyright symbol Also phonogram copyright symbol. The letter 'p' enclosed in a circle ℗, printed on a CD or sound recording to indicate that reproduction of the resource is protected under copyright law

source document The original document from which copies are made

Southeast Asia—Pacific Audiovisual Archives Association SEAPAVAA. An association that provides a regional forum for addressing common issues and concerns related to the collection and preservation of, and provision of access to, the audiovisual heritage of member countries
http://archives.pia.gov.ph/seapavaa/

SPARC Scholarly Publishing and Academic Resources Coalition. An alliance of universities, research libraries, and organizations focused on expanding the dissemination of research information
http://www.sparc.arl.org/

special collection A collection of material that is treated in a special way because of its subject matter, age, value, etc.

special issue An issue of a periodical addressing a special subject or occasion

Special Libraries Association SLA. An organization founded in 1909, with an international membership of information professionals who work in special libraries serving business, research, government, etc. http://www.sla.org/

special library A library focusing on a specialized subject area. Usually maintained by a corporation, association or government agency

special-research library A special library with a research function

specific index An alphabetical list that gives one entry only for each topic mentioned in the schedules, together with synonyms

specific material designation In AACR2, a term indicating the specific class of material—e.g., poster—to which a resource belongs. In RDA, this concept is covered by RDA carrier types. Cf general material designation

spider A program that searches the Web and indexes all the words in the documents it finds. Cf robot, crawler, web spider

spine The part of a book's cover that holds the front and back together

spine label A label that is stuck on the spine of library materials showing the call number

spine title The title on the spine of a book

splice To join two pieces together— e.g., splicing film stock or audio tape

Springshare A library technology company; developers of the LibGuides product and other library software and apps for content management, knowledge sharing, statistics and administration. Cf LibGuides

sprocket A roller in a film projector with teeth along one edge that fit into holes at the edge of the film, to pull the film through the projector

stack capacity The storage capacity of a library's stacks

stack maintenance Keeping books and other resources in a library stack in good order

stacks Also bookstacks 1. The rows of shelves containing a library's collection. 2. An area containing seldom-used library materials, usually accessible only to library staff

standard A published document that sets out the minimum requirements needed to ensure that a product, material or procedure will do the job it is intended to do

Standard Address Number SAN. A unique identification number assigned to an organization in or served by the book trade, particularly those involved in electronic transfer of information
https://www.myidentifiers.com.au/san/main

standard list A list of core resources recommended for inclusion in any library collection of a particular type or size, often published by a library association

standard number An ISBN, ISSN or any other internationally agreed upon standard number that identifies the resource uniquely. Cf identifier

standard subdivision 1. An auxiliary number in Dewey Decimal Classification that represents a standard form or treatment of a subject—e.g., -09 for historical treatment. 2. Also free-floating subdivision. A subheading in Library of Congress Subject Headings that is applied to one or more categories of main headings—e.g., Periodicals

standard work A work recognized as worthy of emulation in its subject or field

standing order Also continuation order, till forbid order. An order for all future issues of a serial title until the publisher is notified that no more issues are required

state library The government-funded library of a state or territory, providing library services to the whole state, including support of public libraries

state library agency In the U.S., an organization authorized by a state government to promote library services in the state through the coordination of a variety of library services. Cf COSLA

state manual Also blue book. A publication by a U.S. state government containing the state charter and/or constitution, election statistics, and other details of the government structure and personnel

statement of responsibility In RDA, a statement that identifies the person(s), family(ies) or corporate body(ies) responsible for the intellectual or artistic content of a resource. Cf multiple statements of responsibility, single statement of responsibility

Stationery Office (UK). *See* The Stationery Office

statutory copy Also deposit copy. A free copy of a publication, sent to a copyright depository by the author or publisher to satisfy a legal requirement

steady state Also zero growth. A library collection in which the number of items added each year is balanced by withdrawing the same number

stemming Searching in which only the stem of the word is looked for, and the result includes every term with the same word stem—e.g., enter quaker and find quake, quaking etc. Cf truncation

stereo, stereophonic Recorded and played back through two separate sound channels. Cf monaural, monophonic

stocktaking Also inventory. Checking the items in the collection, including items on loan, awaiting repair etc., against the complete record of a library's holdings (shelf-list)

stop list The set of stop words of a particular searching system or software

stop word A very common word—e.g., and, but, the—that a computer ignores when searching by keyword

story hour A time set aside for reading and telling stories to a library's young clients

Storylines Children's Literature Foundation and Storylines Trust Formerly the Children's Literature Association of New Zealand and the New Zealand Children's Book Foundation. The New Zealand National Section of IBBY (International Board on Books for Young People), whose aim is to support and promote children's literature in New Zealand. See the Storylines website for their awards and prizes
http://www.storylines.org.nz/

strategic planning Developing long-term objectives, and considering how to achieve them

string searching Matching a sequence of characters within a body of text

student assistant A student in a school or academic institution who is employed part-time in the library

style manual A set of rules designed to ensure consistency of spelling, abbreviations, citation style etc.

style sheet A list of rules of spelling, punctuation, and citation, that a publisher wishes authors to apply in their writing

stylus The needle used to obtain sound from a gramophone record

subdivision A section of a classification scheme or subject heading

subfield 1. Part of the MARC record that contains an element of description or other small piece of information. 2. Part of a field

subfield code The two-character code that precedes a data element in a MARC record—e.g., $a

subfield delimiter The character used to introduce a subfield in a MARC record—e.g., $

subheading A secondary heading added to a subject heading or descriptor

Subito An online interlibrary loan and document delivery service based in Germany, sourcing material mainly from European libraries
http://www.subito-doc.de

subject The theme or themes of a work

Subject Authority Cooperative Program SACO. The subject authority component of the Program for Cooperative Cataloging of the Library of Congress
http://www.loc.gov/aba/pcc/saco/index.html

subject bibliography A publication listing references on a topic

subject cataloging, subject cataloguing Describing the content of a work using subject headings and a classification number

subject encyclopedia, subject encyclopaedia A publication of comprehensive information on a specific subject or field. Cf encyclopedia

subject gateway Also gateway, portal. An entry point to the Internet that provides access to electronic information including websites, ftp sites, databases and indexes to print resources in a specific subject area

subject heading A heading that describes a subject and provides subject access to a catalog

subject specialist A librarian with specialized knowledge of a subject area

subordinate body A part, section or division of a larger corporate body. It is often identified by referring to the parent body

subscription An order for all issues of a serial published within a certain time, usually one or two years. Payment is made in advance for the whole period

subscription agent A person or company that provides services to libraries wanting to purchase serials. Services cover ordering subscriptions, arranging payments and invoicing the library, following up missing issues etc.

subscription work A work that is published only after a sufficient number of purchasers have agreed to cover part of the cost of production

subsidy publishing Also vanity press, vanity publisher. A publisher specializing in producing books entirely at the author's risk and expense

subsystem Part of an integrated system—e.g., the circulation subsystem

subtitle Also other title information. Title on a resource other than the title proper or parallel or series title; also any phrase appearing in conjunction with the title proper

SuDocs number The call number of a U.S. government publication, assigned according to a special classification system maintained by the U.S. Superintendent of Documents—e.g., SBA 1.1/2-2 (Small Business Economic Indicators). Cf FDsys

summary Also abstract. A brief indication of the essential points of an article or literary work

summer reading program A program offered by a school library or the children's section of a public library, to keep children reading during the summer vacation

Summon Discovery layer software by Serials Solution. Cf discovery layer

super record A concept of a catalog record that links all the records of different manifestations of a work into one record

supplement 1. A resource issued separately that brings a monograph up to date or otherwise adds to the work. 2. Extra issues of a serial title

supplier A company whose primary function is to obtain material from publishers and supply it to information agencies

support staff Library employees who perform clerical, technical or maintenance tasks

surrogate 1. A copy of an item, sometimes in another format—e.g., microform, photocopy—generally for preservation. 2. A bibliographic record that represents the resource

Symphony An integrated library management system, developed and distributed by SirsiDynix
http://www.sirsidynix.com/symphony

syndetic Connected by cross references

synoptic journal A journal that publishes only brief reports and abstracts (synopses)

syntax Also search syntax. The order of entering computer search terms, that governs the order in which the operations are carried out

synthetic classification Classification that allows the classifier to construct (synthesize) numbers for composite subjects—e.g., Colon Classification, Universal Decimal Classification

systems integration Combining in-house systems with external systems

systems librarian A librarian who is responsible for a library's hardware and software systems

table A set of numbers in a classification scheme that are added to a number from the schedules to make a more specific number. Cf schedule

table of contents TOC. A list of the contents of a publication, with corresponding page numbers

tag A label that identifies each field of a MARC record—e.g., 245 identifies the title and statement of responsibility field

talking book Also audiobook, book-on-tape. A book that has been read onto audiotape, CD or mp3 player

tattle tape Magnetic tape inserted in a library item that activates an alarm if the item is removed from the library without being checked out

teacher-librarian Also school librarian. A librarian who manages a school library and offers a library service to students and staff of a school

technical processing Also technical services. Library services that deal with the bibliographic control—including acquisition, cataloging and end processing—of library material

technical report A scientific report of research findings

technical services Also technical processing. Library services that deal with the bibliographic control—including acquisition, cataloging and end processing—of library material

TEI Text Encoding Initiative. A consortium that develops and maintains guidelines for the encoding of literary and linguistic texts in electronic form
http://www.tei-c.org/

Te Kaunihera Pukapuka O Aotearoa / New Zealand Book Council An independent, non-profit body established in 1972 to promote and celebrate the love of books and reading
http://www.bookcouncil.org.nz/

teleconferencing Conducting an audio conference between remote sites via telephone lines

temporary copy An electronic copy made for transmission, stored briefly in case the transmission failed and it needs to be sent again, then deleted to comply with copyright regulations

Te Patakataka A simplified edition of the Dewey Decimal Classification developed by the National Library of New Zealand for elementary schools
http://www.natlib.govt.nz/

Te Puna A subscription-based information access tool for libraries, managed by the National Library of New Zealand. Includes the holdings of New Zealand libraries, provides access to the National Library's databases such as Index New Zealand, and offers sophisticated cataloging and interloan services
http://natlib.govt.nz/librarians/te-puna

Te Puna Interloan A web-based interlibrary loan management system for the request and supply of resources between libraries, managed by the National Library of New Zealand. Cf New Zealand Interlibrary Loan Scheme
http://tepuna.natlib.govt.nz/about/ill.htm

Te Puna Mātauranga o Aoteoroa / National Library of New Zealand Government-funded cultural and information centre, whose role is to collect and maintain literature and resources that relate to New Zealand and the Pacific, to make this information readily available, and to preserve New Zealand's documentary heritage for future generations
http://www.natlib.govt.nz

Te Puna National Bibliography *See* New Zealand National Bibliography

Te Rarangi Puranga, Tuhinga Ake o te Motu / New Zealand National Register of Archives and Manuscripts *See* The Community Archive

Te Rau Herenga o Aotearoa / Library and Information Association of New Zealand Aoteroa LIANZA. The professional body in New Zealand for those engaged in librarianship and information management. It actively promotes the use and development of libraries and information service through publications, meetings, continuing education programs and conferences
http://www.lianza.org.nz

terms of availability Terms on which the item is available, including price or other statement

Te Rōpō Whakahau The professional association for New Zealand Maori who work in libraries, archives and information services
http://www.trw.org.nz/

Te Ropu Tautoko I Te Puna Matauranga / National Library Society A society formed to strengthen the links between the National Library of New Zealand and the community, and to support the National Library to achieve its goals
http://nationallibrarysociety.org.nz/

tertiary source A guide to the literature of a particular field—e.g., a bibliography of bibliographies, a directory of directories, etc.

Te Rua Mahara o te Kawanatanga / Archives New Zealand The organization that ensures access to and preservation of New Zealand government records
http://www.archives.govt.nz/

tête-bêche A work with text in one language and the same text in another language when the work is turned upside-down

Text Encoding Initiative TEI. A consortium that develops and maintains guidelines for the encoding of literary and linguistic texts in electronic form
http://www.tei-c.org/

text to speech software Computer programs that convert an e-book, word-processed file or other written text to phonetic sound and 'read' it back using simulated speech

Theatre Library Association. A U.S. organization that supports librarians and archivists affiliated with theatre, dance, performance studies, popular entertainment, motion picture and broadcasting collections
http://www.tla-online.org/

The Community Archive Formerly *New Zealand National Register of Archives and Manuscripts*. A register of archival collections held in museums, local government bodies, libraries, historical societies, community repositories, and in-house business, educational, religious and sporting archives throughout New Zealand
http://thecommunityarchive.org.nz/

The Stationery Office TSO. A private company responsible for publishing and distributing British government publications since 1996, when it took over this role from Her Majesty's Stationery Office
https://www.tso.co.uk/

thesaurus 1. A work containing synonymous and related words and phrases. 2. A list of controlled terms used in a database

thesis Also dissertation. A treatise prepared for the award of a diploma or degree, especially a postgraduate degree

third summary of Dewey Decimal Classification The 1000 sections, each of which is a whole number, and represents a specific topic

Thomson Reuters A commercial organization that offers access to online and CD-ROM databases, mainly in legal and financial services
http://www.thomsonreuters.com.au/

thumb drive Also flash drive, memory stick, USB flash drive. A removable and rewritable data storage device, used for storage, backup and transfer of computer files. Often used in preference to CD-ROMs because of its high storage capacity, small size, durability and reliability. Cf CD-ROM

thumbnail A small image that represents the same image in larger format

TIFF Tagged image file format. A graphic file format widely used for scanned images

tilde 1. The symbol ~ used when formulating a search strategy in some library databases to search for synonyms. Cf Boolean operator. 2. The symbol ~ used to indicate a person's home directory or home page on the Web

till forbid order Also continuation order, standing order. An order for all future issues of a serial title until the publisher is notified that no more issues are required

tipped in (A single sheet) glued into a book with adhesive on the inside edge of the page

title 1. A word or phrase that names a resource. 2. The entire resource, as in 'a number of titles'

title page The page in a printed resource that provides the most complete information about the author and title, and is used as a primary source of cataloging data

title proper The main name of a resource, including alternative title(s) but excluding parallel titles and other title information

TOC table of contents. A list of the contents of a publication, with corresponding page numbers

tome A volume or book, especially a heavy one

topical 1. Relating to matters of interest of the day. 2. Relating to a subject

topical guide Also pathfinder. Directions to the resources available for a literature search. Cf LibGuides

traced series A series for which an added entry is made

tracing, tracing note A record of the headings under which a resource is entered in a catalog

trade bibliography, trade catalog, trade list A listing of books available for sale in a country, together with details of publishers etc. needed for purchase

trade journal A periodical of interest to a specific industry or trade

transaction log A record of the use of a (usually electronic) information source

transaction processing Also real-time processing. Processing that updates information immediately. Cf batch processing

transcribe In RDA cataloging, copying exactly the details that are seen on a resource (including any errors) into a bibliographic record

transcript 1. A written record or copy. 2. A written copy of a speech or electronic document

transcription (v) The process of making a written record or copy. (n) *See* transcript

translation A work rendered in another language

transliteration Rendering of the letters or characters of one alphabet into those of another—e.g., romanization

Trans Tasman Interlending A service linking Te Puna Interloan and Libraries Australia Document Delivery, to support document delivery for Australia and New Zealand

trap A procedure in a circulation system that interrupts certain transactions—e.g., not allowing a borrower to borrow a not-for-loan item

TRIM *See* HP Records Manager.

Trove A discovery service for Australia, Australians and items found in Australian collecting institutions, developed by the National Library of Australia. It includes the bibliographic records of Libraries Australia as well as newspaper, theses, research, picture, music, archival and biographical databases formerly maintained by the National Library. It also acts as a social network, where users can create and share lists, tag items, and correct newspaper texts
http://trove.nla.gov.au/

truncation Abbreviation of a search term using a special symbol, such as #, *, in order to include variants of the term such as plurals, adjectives etc. Cf stemming, wild card

TSO The Stationery Office. A private company responsible for publishing and distributing British government publications since 1996, when it took over this role from Her Majesty's Stationery Office
https://www.tso.co.uk/

tuner A radio that needs to be connected to an amplifier and speakers

turnaround time 1. The time between starting and completing a computer operation. Cf response time. 2. The time between requesting and receiving an interlibrary loan

typescript (adj) Written on a typewriter. (n) A typed manuscript

UCC Universal Copyright Convention. An international convention that came into effect in 1955, and provides reciprocal protection of copyright in the member countries simply by using the symbol ©, the name of the copyright owner and the year of first publication
http://www.wipo.int/wipolex/en/other_treaties/details.jsp?treaty_id=208

UDC Universal Decimal Classification. A classification scheme developed by the International Federation for Information and Documentation (FID) by expanding Dewey Decimal Classification. It offers the most specific classification for specialized collections and is widely used in special libraries

UF Used For. A term to introduce a non-preferred term for a subject or name, to refer users to a preferred term

UKMARC The machine-readable cataloging format developed by the British Library ; replaced by MARC 21

UKOLN Informatics Formerly U.K. Office for Library and Information Networking. A national centre for support in network information management in the library and information communities, providing awareness, research and information services. From 2013, based at the University of Bath

ULC Urban Libraries Council. An association of public library systems in metropolitan areas of the U.S. and Canada, advocating the value of libraries as change agents that transform communities
http://www.urbanlibraries.org/

ULL uploading, upline loading. Copying data (e.g., bibliographic records) from one's own computer to a remote database (e.g., WorldCat). Cf DLL

Ulrich's International Periodical Directory Trade bibliography for serials. Lists all current serials published anywhere in the world. Available in print from Bowker and online as Ulrichsweb from ProQuest's Serials Solutions

ultrafiche Ultra microfiche. Microfiche with extremely small images, allowing more material to be reproduced on a single piece of fiche

unabridged Not shortened

unbound Not bound (with other issues of the periodical to form a volume)

uncontrolled Not verified in an authority file

undergraduate library A university library that serves the information and research needs of its undergraduate students and teaching programs

unexpurgated Complete, including passages omitted from other editions on grounds of offensiveness

UNICODE A standard for character-encoding; an international character code to enable coding of the main scripts of the world, including non-roman scripts

uniform edition A series of books printed and bound in the same style

Uniform Resource Locator URL. The address of a site on the World Wide Web

Uniform Resource Name URN. A unique, stable, location-independent identifier for an object or service, for example ISBN, ISSN. Generally consists of a string containing the naming authority and the string—e.g., ISBN/082478431X

uniform title An AACR2 cataloging concept, with different definitions for monographs and serials. RDA uses 'preferred title of a work' as a similar, but not exactly equivalent concept. 1. In AACR2 cataloging, a title chosen to identify a monograph appearing under varying titles—e.g., Bible. 2. In AACR2 cataloging, a title used to distinguish the heading for one serial or series from the heading for another serial or series—e.g., Bulletin (UNESCO)

UNIMARC UNIversal MAchine-Readable Cataloging. The version of the MARC format for cataloging bibliographic items developed by IFLA, widely used in Europe and now maintained by the National Library of Portugal. Cf MARC 21

union catalog, union catalogue Catalog of the holdings of more than one library

unique call number A number on a library item consisting of a classification number, a book number and often a location symbol, that is different from every other call number in the library

United States Government Printing Office USGPO. The U.S. Government publishing and sales organization for federal government publications http://www.gpo.gov/

Universal Copyright Convention UCC. An international convention that came into effect in 1955, and provides reciprocal protection of copyright in the member countries simply by using the symbol ©, the name of the copyright owner and the year of first publication
http://www.wipo.int/wipolex/en/other_treaties/details.jsp?treaty_id=208

Universal Decimal Classification UDC. A classification scheme developed by the International Federation for Information and Documentation (FID) by expanding Dewey Decimal Classification. It offers the most specific classification for specialized collections and is widely used in special libraries

UNIversal MAchine-Readable Cataloging UNIMARC. The version of the MARC format for cataloging bibliographic items developed by IFLA, widely used in Europe and now maintained by the National Library of Portugal. Cf MARC21

university library A library or library system established by a university to meet the needs of its students, faculty, and staff

university press A publishing house associated with a university, which publishes scholarly books and periodicals

unmediated One of RDA's 'media types', used to indicate types of resources (texts, objects, etc.) that do not require equipment to view

unmediated search A search performed by an end-user without the authorization or assistance of a library

untraced series A series for which no added entry is made

unzip To decompress a compressed file so that it can be manipulated by a computer

updated version A new version of a work from which obsolete information has been removed and current information substituted

updating loose-leaf An integrating resource consisting of one or more base volumes that are updated by adding, removing and/or substituting pages. Cf loose-leaf publication

upline loading, uploading ULL. Copying data (e.g., bibliographic records) from one's own computer to a remote database (e.g., WorldCat). Cf downline loading

upper-case Capital letter (e.g., A, B, C). Cf lower-case

Urban Libraries Council ULC. An association of public library systems in metropolitan areas of the U.S. and Canada, advocating the value of libraries as change agents that transform communities
http://www.urbanlibraries.org/

URL Uniform Resource Locator. The address of a site on the World Wide Web

URN Uniform Resource Name. A unique, stable, location-independent identifier for an object or service, for example ISBN, ISSN. Generally contains the naming authority and the string—e.g., ISBN/082478431X

USA.gov The U.S. federal government's official web portal, with comprehensive information on government resources and services
http://www.usa.gov/

USB flash drive Also flash drive, memory stick, thumb drive. A removable and rewritable data storage device, used for storage, backup and transfer of computer files. Often used in preference to CD-ROMs because of its high storage capacity, small size, durability and reliability. Cf CD-ROM

user Also client, patron. A person who uses the services of a library

user education Also bibliographic instruction, client education, library orientation, reader education, reader instruction. Helping people to derive the most benefit from using the library

user group 1. The categories or types of people who make regular use of a library's services and collections. 2. The users of particular software or hardware, organized to share experiences, improve their understanding of the product, and communicate ideas about it—e.g., Horizon Users Group

user pays A situation in which a client (including organizations, government departments etc.) pays for services provided by an information agency

user tasks The key functions that users expect a catalog to help them with. FRBR and RDA identify the user tasks for bibliographic records as find, identify, select and obtain (FISO), and for authority records as find, identify, justify or clarify and contextualize or understand (FIJC, FICU)

USGPO United States Government Printing Office. The U.S. Government publishing and sales organization for federal government publications
http://www.gpo.gov/

USMARC Library of Congress machine-readable cataloging format, known as LCMARC until the 1980s. Harmonized with Canadian MARC to create MARC 21 in the late 1990s

VALA—Libraries, Technology and the Future Inc. Australian organization that promotes the use of information technology in libraries and the broader information sector, and biennially hosts the largest library technology conference in Australia
http://www.vala.org.au/

Validator A commercial database on DVD of Library of Congress subject and names authorities records, updated quarterly
http://www.lssi.com/services/library-data-services/validator/

valuable consideration A fee

vanity press, vanity publisher Also subsidy publishing. A publisher specializing in producing books entirely at the author's risk and expense

Vanuatu Cultural Centre The centre concerned with Vanuatu's history, languages, library, museum, film and sound collections, policies and projects
http://www.vanuatuculture.org/

Vanuatu National Library The national library collections & service of Vanuatu
http://www.vanuatuculture.org/site-bm2/library/050517_nationallibrary.shtml

variable control field A field in a MARC record with a tag 001-009 and no indicators or subfield codes. Control fields contain coded data used in processing the record

variable field A field containing either control or bibliographic data

variable length field A field that does not have its length determined in advance, and is therefore only as long as it needs to be. Cf fixed length field

variant access point In RDA cataloging, a non-preferred variation of a title or name. Known as a 'see reference' in AACR2, it provides a direction from an access point that is not used to an authorized access point that is used. Cf authorized access point

variant edition An edition that includes textual changes made by the author

variant title A different form of the title

VCR videocassette recorder. Equipment that enables videorecordings to be made and played back

VDX Virtual Document Exchange. Interlibrary loan management software from OCLC, used by library networks and consortia
https://oclc.org/vdx/about.en.html

vendor A company that provides serials, supplies, library systems, databases, and other products and services for a fee

verification Checking data to confirm bibliographic details

vernacular The native speech or language of a place

version A different edition, manifestation or adaptation of a work

verso The left-hand page of an open book; the back of a leaf of a book—e.g., verso of the title page. Cf recto

vertical file A collection of current material including pamphlets and newspaper clippings. Usually arranged in subject order in a filing cabinet

vesicular microfilm A form of microfilm in which the image is contained in bubbles within the film, protecting the image from damage

VI Visible index. A manual file of all the information about a library's serials

VIAF Virtual International Authority File. A cooperative project of national libraries and organizations, to develop an online international authority file by linking national personal name authority files. Hosted by OCLC
http://viaf.org/

videocassette recorder VCR. Equipment that enables videorecordings to be made and played back

video conferencing A means of providing audio and video communication between remote sites in order to conduct a meeting or conference

videotape Strip of mylar plastic tape covered with iron oxide that can be magnetized. Sound and pictures are encoded as magnetic signals

vinyl record Also gramophone record, phonograph record. A sound disc made of vinyl plastic, with sound grooves pressed into the surface

vinyl tape Non-acidic plastic tape used to cover and repair library material

Virtual Document Exchange VDX. Interlibrary loan management software from OCLC, used by library networks and consortia
https://oclc.org/vdx/about.en.html

Virtual International Authority File VIAF. A cooperative project of national libraries and organizations, to develop an online international authority file by linking national personal name authority files. Hosted by OCLC
http://viaf.org/

virtual library A library whose primary resources are electronic, and that provides access for its users to databases, images etc., including via other information providers

virtual reference services Also digital reference services, ask a librarian services. Reference assistance by library professionals, given online to library clients who may email, post questions, submit reference forms or engage in interactive chats or instant messaging

VISCOPY The Australian and New Zealand rights management organization for the visual arts, providing copyright licensing services for the use of visual art works
http://www.viscopy.org.au/about

visible index VI. A manual file of all the information about a library's serials

volume 1. What is contained in one binding of a monograph. 2. A number of issues of a serial, usually those published in one twelve-month period

Voyager An integrated library management system designed for large academic and research libraries or consortia
http://www.exlibrisgroup.com/category/Voyager

Wade Giles System of romanization of Chinese characters

waiting list 1. Also want list, desiderata. A list of books and other materials wanted by a library, to be accepted when offered, or purchased when funds are available. 2. A list of library patrons who have placed a reserve on a resource, indicating the order in which they will be allocated the resource when it becomes available

wall shelving Shelving placed against or fixed to a wall. Cf free-standing shelving

want list Also desiderata, waiting list. A list of books and other materials wanted by a library, to be accepted when offered, or purchased when funds are available

warping The bending or twisting out of shape of a book cover after binding

Warwick Framework An architecture for use with Dublin Core, developed at the Warwick Metadata Workshop in 1996, designed for the exchange of metadata packages by aggregating metadata packages into containers

watermark Also papermark. 1. A faint mark that can be seen in a sheet of good quality paper. 2. A design or lettering printed in grey across a page

WBIS Online World Biographical Information System Online. A De Gruyter subscription database of biographical information published in reference works from the 16th century to the present, based on the digitization of the KG Saur Verlag's *World Biographical Archives System* microfiche
http://www.degruyter.com/view/serial/35520?rskey=50HF44&result=4

WCT WIPO Copyright Treaty. An international treaty concluded in 1996 to protect intellectual creations of new technology, especially computer programs and databases that constitute intellectual creations
http://www.wipo.int/treaties/en/ip/wct/index.html

Web Also World Wide Web, WWW. A collection of sites on the Internet in which users can move easily from one document or site to another by means of hypertext links

web browser Computer software that enables users to access the World Wide Web, and move from one site, document etc. to another—e.g., Internet Explorer, Firefox, Safari, Google Chrome

web conferencing Also webinar, online workshop. Conferences, seminars, workshops and other interactive online conferencing events that can be shared simultaneously across geographically dispersed locations, often via web conferencing services that use cloud computing technologies

web crawler Also web robot, web spider. A software robot that trawls the Web, generating all-encompassing web indexes

web directory A web search tool in which websites are collected and evaluated by human beings, and organized under appropriate subject headings or categories—e.g., Yahoo!, Infomine, DMOZ

webinar Also web conferencing, online workshop. Conferences, seminars, workshops and other interactive online conferencing events that can be shared simultaneously across geographically dispersed locations, often via web conferencing services that use cloud computing technologies

web robot, web spider Also web crawler. A software robot that trawls the Web, generating all-encompassing web indexes

web-zine Also e-zine, zine. An online magazine or newsletter, distributed by email or posted on a website

weed, weeding Also deselection. Discarding resources that are considered to be of no further use to the library, and removing their catalog records

weekly Issued once a week

WEMI The acronym used to describe RDA's Group I entities: Work, Expression, Manifestation, Item

white paper An official government report, stating either government policy or where the government wishes to go on an issue. Cf green paper

WHS workplace health and safety. Also EH&S, environmental health and safety, OH&S, occupational health and safety. Legal requirements for ensuring a safe workplace

Wi-Fi Wireless Fidelity A high speed Internet and network connection using high frequency radio waves, that allows computers, smartphones and other devices to connect to the Internet or communicate with each other wirelessly

Wiki 1. Server software that allows users freely to create and edit web page content using any web browser. 2. A website or database developed collaboratively by a community of users, allowing any user to add or edit content. 3. (v) to research a topic on a wiki, or to contribute to a wiki http://www.wiki.com/

Wikipedia A multilingual, web-based free content encyclopedia, written collaboratively by volunteers and allowing most articles to be changed by almost anyone with access to the website http://wikipedia.org/

wild card A symbol that replaces one character in a search term — e.g., organi#ation. Cf truncation

WILU Workshop for Instruction in Library Use. A major Canadian conference where delegates meet to discuss topics related to information literacy, held annually since 1972

WIPO World Intellectual Property Organization. An intergovernmental organization responsible for the promotion of the protection of intellectual property throughout the world, and for the administration of multilateral treaties dealing with legal and administrative aspects of intellectual property http://www.wipo.org

WIPO Copyright Treaty WCT. An international treaty concluded in 1996 to protect intellectual creations of new technology, especially computer programs and databases that constitute intellectual creations http://www.wipo.int/treaties/en/ip/wct/index.html

WIPO Performances and Phonograms Treaty WPPT. An international treaty concluded in 1996 to protect the intellectual property rights of performers (actors, singers, musicians, etc.), and producers of phonograms http://www.wipo.int/treaties/en/ip/wppt/index.html

wireless OPAC The ability to search a library's catalog on tablet computers or mobile phones

withdrawal 1. Removing an item from a library collection. 2. Deleting a record from the catalog when the item it represents has been lost or discarded

word-by-word alphabetization, word-by-word alphabetisation Arranging in strict alphabetical order within each word—e.g., New Town before newness. Cf letter-by-letter alphabetization

work In RDA, one of the Group 1 entities described in *Functional Requirements for Bibliographic Records* as representing the initial intellectual or artistic creation—e.g., the concept that becomes Shakespeare's *Hamlet*. Cf expression, item, manifestation

work experience Also practicum (American usage). A period of work in an information agency to gain practical experience

workflow 1. The sequence in which work is passed from one work area to another. 2. In RDA, the documentation created by catalogers indicating their procedures for cataloging types of resources (similar to 'cheat sheets')

work mark A letter used in Cutter-Sanborn numbers to distinguish different titles by the same author

workplace health and safety WHS. Also EH&S, environmental health and safety, OH&S, occupational health and safety. Legal requirements for ensuring a safe workplace

Workshop for Instruction in Library Use WILU. A major Canadian conference where delegates meet to discuss topics related to information literacy, held annually since 1972

workstation 1. A desktop computer configured to perform a specific function, such as searching online databases, cataloging. 2. A work or office area outfitted for one person, and usually including a computer

World Biographical Information System Online WBIS Online. A De Gruyter subscription database of the biographical information published in reference works from the 16th century to the present, based on the digitization of the KG Saur Verlag's *World Biographical Archives System* microfiche
http://www.degruyter.com/view/serial/35520?rskey=50HF44&result=4

WorldCat OCLC's bibliographic database with records from over 9000 libraries
http://www.oclc.org/worldcat/

World Intellectual Property Organization WIPO. An intergovernmental organization responsible for the promotion of the protection of intellectual property throughout the world, and for the administration of multilateral treaties dealing with legal and administrative aspects of intellectual property
http://www.wipo.org

World Wide Web Also the Web, WWW. A collection of sites on the Internet in which users can move easily from one document or site to another by means of hypertext links

WPPT WIPO Performances and Phonograms Treaty. An international treaty concluded in 1996 to protect the intellectual property rights of performers (actors, singers, musicians, etc.), and producers of phonograms
http://www.wipo.int/treaties/en/ip/wppt/index.html

wrapper Also book jacket, dust cover, dust jacket, dust wrapper, jacket. Paper cover for a hard-bound book

Yahoo Search An early search engine still widely used, particularly in the U.S.
http://www.yahoo.com;   http://au.yahoo.com/

yearbook An annual publication containing current information in brief, descriptive and/or statistical form

young adult book A book intended to be read by adolescents

young adult services Library services for adolescents

Z39.50 A client/server-based information retrieval protocol for library applications, designed to aid retrieval from distributed servers. Issued by the American National Standards Institute/National Information Standards Organization (ANSI/NISO Z39.50)
http://www.niso.org/standards/resources/Z39.50_Resources

Z39.50 compliant Meeting the specifications of the Z39.50 protocol, so that information can be retrieved from most library databases

Z39.50 target A server that supports the Z39.50 standard

zero-based budgeting Financial planning that requires managers to evaluate all their programs each year and to budget as if they were starting from scratch, or base zero, for the coming year's costs

zero growth Also steady state. A library collection in which the number of items added each year is balanced by withdrawing the same number

zine Also e-zine, web-zine. An online magazine or newsletter, distributed by email or posted on a website

Zinio for Libraries A commercial service that allows public libraries to grant patrons access to selected digital magazines, viewable via the patron's web browser, smartphone or tablet device
http://www.zinio.com

zip To compress a file so that it takes up less space on a disc. Cf data compression

Bibliography

American Library Association, Canadian Library Association and CILIP: Chartered Institute of Library and Information Professionals, *RDA Toolkit*. Viewed March 2014
http://www.rdatoolkit.org/

Domenico, Dave, *Library lingo: a glossary of library terminology*. (a web publication by Colorado State University Libraries). Viewed March 2014
http://lib.colostate.edu/lingo

IFLA glossary of terms and abbreviations and useful links. Viewed March 2014
http://www.ifla.org/node/7666

Jones, David J., *The Australian dictionary of acronyms and abbreviations*. 6th edition, Canberra, ALIA Press, 2005

Keenan, Stella and Colin Johnston, *Concise dictionary of library and information science*. 2nd edition, London, Bowker-Saur, 2000

Levine-Clark and Carter, Toni M, editors, *ALA Glossary of library and information science*. 4th edition, Chicago, ALA Editions, 2013

Prytherch, Ray, *Harrod's librarians' glossary and reference book: a directory of over 10,200 terms, organizations, projects, and acronyms in the areas of information management, library science, publishing, and archive management*. 10th edition, Aldershot, Gower, 2005

Reitz, Joan M., *ODLIS: online dictionary for library and information science*. Viewed April 2014
http://www.abc-clio.com/ODLIS/odlis_A.aspx

Stevenson, Janet, *Dictionary of library and information management*. 2nd edition, London, A & C Black, 2006

TechEncyclopedia. Viewed April 2014
http://www.techweb.com/encyclopedia/

The Macquarie dictionary. 5th edition, North Ryde, N.S.W., Macquarie Dictionary Publishers, 2009

University of California Berkeley Library, *Glossary of Internet & web jargon*. Viewed April 2014
http://www.lib.berkeley.edu/TeachingLib/Guides/Internet/Glossary.html

and the websites of the many organizations included in LibrarySpeak

Feedback Please

Inevitably, a glossary like this contains errors, and useful terms have been missed. New terms will also be added to our professional vocabulary between now and the next edition.

In attempting to cover new developments for this edition, particularly in the international sphere, I have relied heavily on the Web. I am aware of the limitations of this approach, and would welcome information from people with greater regional knowledge than mine to supplement my research.

There are also likely to be some out-of-date terms. These should be identified and deleted, to keep *LibrarySpeak* to a manageable size.

If you have any suggestions for the next edition, please send them to:

LibrarySpeak
c/- Lynn Farkas
PO Box 7068
Farrer ACT 2607
Australia
Email: farkastraining@gmail.com

Thank you.

LEARN LIBRARY SKILLS SERIES

This series of paperback workbooks introduces skills needed by library science students and library technicians, as well as librarians seeking refresher materials or study guides for in-service training classes. Each book teaches essential professional skills in a step-by-step process, accompanied by numerous practical examples, exercises and quizzes to reinforce learning, and an appropriate glossary.

Learn About Information
International Edition ©2015
Helen Rowe
ISBN: 9781590954331 Paperback

Learn Basic Library Skills
International Edition ©2015
Helen Rowe and Trina Grover
ISBN: 9781590954348 Paperback

Learn Cataloging the RDA way
International Edition ©2015
Lynn Farkas and Helen Rowe
ISBN: 9781590954355 Paperback

Learn Dewey Decimal Classification (Edition 23)
International Edition ©2015
Lynn Farkas
ISBN: **9781590954362** Paperback

Learn Management Skills for Libraries and Information Agencies
International Edition ©2015
Jacinta Ganendran
ISBN: 9781590954379 Paperback

Learn Library of Congress Classification
International Edition ©2015
ISBN: 9781590954386 Paperback

Learn Library of Congress Subject Access
International Edition ©2015
Lynn Farkas
ISBN 9781590954393 Paperback

Learn Reference Work
International Edition ©2015
ISBN: 9781590954416 Paperback

LIBRARY SCIENCE TITLES

LibrarySpeak:
A Glossary of Terms in Librarianship and Information Technology,
International Edition ©2015
Lynn Farkas
ISBN: 9781590954423 Paperback

My Mentoring Diary:
A Resource for the Library and Information Professions
Revised Edition ©2015
Ann Ritchie and Paul Genoni
ISBN: 9781590954430 Paperback

Quality in Library Service:
A Competency-Based Staff Training Program
International Edition ©2015
Jennifer Burrell and Brad McGrath
ISBN: 9781590954447 Paperback

TOTALRECALL PUBLICATIONS, INC.
1103 Middlecreek,
Friendswood, TX 77546-5448

Phone: (281) 992-3131
email: Sales@TotalRecallPress.com
Online: www.totalrecallpress.com

Notes:

www.ingramcontent.com/pod-product-compliance
Lightning Source LLC
Chambersburg PA
CBHW081102070526
44584CB00021B/3175